"In this engaging theological reflection, Mark McIntosh and Frank Griswold enter into the 'conversation of true friends' that urges us, in turn, to travel further into friendship with God in Christ. For the authors, God is the source of our true self, discovered through ongoing conversion and transformation. This fine book invites us to share in Jesus's own self-giving love for the sake of others, as he draws us into his own relationship with the Father."

— JOHN C. BAUERSCHMIDT
bishop of the Episcopal Diocese of Tennessee

"Two contemporary Abbas explore afresh an array of traditional Christian faith claims: creation and redemption, suffering and evil, Christology and reconciliation, death and the life to come. In concert with voices from across church history, they forge a path towards a mystic Christian spirituality for the future. Learned yet accessible, this volume will be a blessing for both individual and parish formation. A gem."

— KATHRYN GREENE-MCCREIGHT
priest affiliate at Christ Church, New Haven, Connecticut

"Thomas Merton once said that it is a disaster to separate theology from spirituality. In *Seeds of Faith*, Mark McIntosh and Bishop Frank Griswold show us how to bring these two essential dimensions of faith together again. This is a book that will bring insights to your mind and inspiration to your heart."

— CARL MCCOLMAN
author of *Unteachable Lessons* and *Eternal Heart*

T0287097

Seeds of Faith

*Theology and Spirituality
at the Heart of Christian Belief*

Mark A. McIntosh
Frank T. Griswold

WILLIAM B. EERDMANS PUBLISHING COMPANY
GRAND RAPIDS, MICHIGAN

Wm. B. Eerdmans Publishing Co.

4035 Park East Court SE, Grand Rapids, Michigan 49546

www.eerdmans.com

Published 2022

Printed in the United States of America

28 27 26 25 24 23 22   1 2 3 4 5 6 7

ISBN 978-0-8028-7973-8

Library of Congress Cataloging-in-Publication Data

Names: McIntosh, Mark Allen, 1960– author. | Griswold,
      Frank T., 1937– author.
Title: Seeds of faith : theology and spirituality at the heart of
      Christian belief / Mark A. McIntosh, Frank T. Griswold.
Description: Grand Rapids, Michigan : William B. Eerdmans
      Publishing Company, [2022] | Includes index. | Summary:
      "An introduction to Christian doctrine that prioritizes a
      mutually reinforcing relationship between theology and
      spirituality" — Provided by publisher.
Identifiers: LCCN 2021055334 | ISBN 9780802879738
Subjects: LCSH: Theology. | Theology, Doctrinal. |
      Spirituality — Christianity. | BISAC: RELIGION /
      Christian Theology / General | RELIGION / Mysticism
Classification: LCC BR118 .M289 2022 |
      DDC 230 — dc23/eng/20220126
LC record available at https://lccn.loc.gov/2021055334

Contents

Acknowledgments   vii

Friends in the Spirit   ix

As We Begin   1

1. The Hidden Presence of God in All Things   7

2. Faith and Fear   21

3. Revelation   32

4. The Mystery of the Trinity   41

5. Creation   51

6. Suffering and Evil   63

7. Jesus as the Incarnate Word   72

8. The Death and Resurrection of Jesus   82

9. Salvation   96

10. Grace and Human Flourishing 111

11. The Church and the Sacramental Life 121

12. The Spirit of Prayer 139

13. Death and the Life to Come 155

14. The Communion of Saints and Mary 166

Index of Subjects 179

Index of Scripture 185

Acknowledgments

These two companion volumes, *Seeds of Faith* and *Harvest of Hope*, would not have been possible without the profound gift to me of Bishop Frank Griswold's spiritual teaching and friendship. His written contributions to these volumes will give readers a sense of the immense generosity of his vision. Our written words, however, are much more likely to make sense to you, and convey more of what we long to share with you, because of the inestimable gifts and contributions of Barbara Braver, our editorial consultant, who, with bountiful good humor and wisdom, has labored to bring words to life and meaning to clarity. I cannot thank her enough for all her help in bringing these volumes to fruition.

It also gives me great joy to thank my beloved wife, Anne, who has helped me in more ways than I can ever express. Living in the later stages of ALS, I have been so wonderfully blessed by her gracious, loving patience and all her efforts to make this season in my life fruitful and hopeful. And our daughter and son, Liza and Nate, have by their encouragement and affection inspired me to keep moving toward the best that I could do.

Mark A. McIntosh

When Mark, in the early stages of ALS, a disease that has now drawn him from this life into Eternity, invited me to help him bring these two volumes into being, I said I would be honored to assist him in any way he might determine. I could think of no better way to express my gratitude for the many years of our friendship, and also for Mark's theological vision, nourished by a life of prayer, which have been an incalculable gift to me and to countless others and permeate these pages. Whether in the classroom or in the pulpit, at the altar or in spiritual counsel, his profoundly pastoral heart and sensitivity of spirit made the love of God and our life in the Trinity intensely real and immediate. These volumes are very much Mark's books, and it has been my joy to add my own voice along the way, usually in response to what Mark has written. As various versions of what became *Seeds of Faith* and *Harvest of Hope* were circulated back and forth, it became clear that we needed a trained eye to read and assess what we were writing. At that point, perhaps the most useful thing I did to further the project was to suggest that we ask Barbara Braver to serve as our editorial consultant. Barbara worked with me during my years as presiding bishop, and her fine mind and clear eye saved me on more than one occasion when a flight of cosmic abstraction in an address or homily needed to be reeled in and rendered in a more assessable form. With Mark, I thank her for her encouragement and wisdom, and for her generous and careful attention to our words and what we were seeking to express.

Frank T. Griswold

Friends in the Spirit

In the early days of my conception of these two volumes, I had two desires: to share with readers my sense of God's all-embracing love through the Trinity, and to share my thoughts in a conversation with a very dear friend who helped me and many others to become aware that our lives *are* always embraced within the Trinitarian love of God. That friend is Bishop Frank Griswold, whom I have known since he was elected bishop of Chicago in 1985. In 1986 he led a retreat for those of us about to be ordained and presided at my ordination to the priesthood. Like most newly ordained clergy, I was passionate about many things when I first met Frank. I'm pretty sure that my certainties veiled (at least from my own heart) my inner confusions and anxieties. But through his presence and teaching, Frank reoriented my soul. And my own experience of his spiritual wisdom was echoed throughout the Diocese of Chicago. It is a little hard to describe how this worked: as I think back on those years, I realize how easily my spiritual being could have been stunted or misdirected had it not been for Frank. Perhaps the simplest way of putting it is to say that

he conveyed to us, in ways almost none of us had experienced
before, the reality of the spiritual world.

Over the next several years, during retreats Frank led and in
sermons he preached, he opened the way for me and countless
others to sense the dimensions of the spiritual world in which
we all really live. As a spiritual teacher, Frank offered examples
from his own life (often humorously self-deprecating) as well as
wisdom from the saints, all of which helped us to notice God's
ways in our lives and to respond with trust and gratitude.

Two spiritual traditions were and are particularly significant in Frank's life and teaching. From his long-standing
friendship with Benedictine communities, Frank was at one
with the spiritual attentiveness at the heart of Saint Benedict's
teaching. God's ever-present word of life is always communicating wisdom and love, if only we can open the ear of our
heart to receive this life-giving presence.

From his own times of regular retreat with Jesuit communities, and his extensive training as a conductor of the *Spiritual
Exercises* of Saint Ignatius Loyola, Frank has always offered all
of us a life-transforming spiritual vision. The foundation of
this vision lies in the deep and ever-renewable sense that God
is continually creating and loving us into existence, and that
our whole lives are being drawn forward into Christ.

Given that over our many years together I have been
blessed and shaped by Frank's mediation of the full force of
God's grace, my very deep desire from the beginning has been
that these volumes would reflect some of Frank's wisdom —
through his words and his reflections on my offerings. Happily,
he agreed with enthusiasm to write reflections on my efforts
and also to put forth some of his own ways of understanding
God's love and action in the world. Thus, these volumes are

a collaboration — something of a conversation. We both very much hope you will join us in this conversation. As the twelfth-century monk and theologian Aelred of Rievaulx observes in his discussion of spiritual friendship, God the Holy Spirit is present in the conversation of true friends. This has been the experience of our friendship over many decades as we have engaged in conversation from our hearts and been blessed by the presence of the Holy Spirit.

In the pages of this book we continue our conversation and invite your spiritual companionship. Perhaps your spiritual friends will join us as we companion one another in these times.

As I write these words, I am in the later stages of ALS: most of my body is paralyzed, but I am still able to speak and swallow. Frank's presence and teaching in my life have helped me to ask Christ, again and again, to give me his love, to let me know that he is always with me, and to make the offering within me of my entire being to the Father. I hope you can understand now why it means so much to me that Frank has generously agreed to be my partner in this undertaking. It is my prayer, and belief, that his voice, emerging here and there throughout the book, will help you to move more deeply and authentically into the goodness and truth God desires to pour out within you as you read.

Mark A. McIntosh

In 1985 when I was elected bishop of Chicago, Mark was serving as assistant at the cathedral, and it was quickly apparent that we shared similar views and had been shaped theologically by the Catholic tradition within Anglicanism. We had both read theology at Oxford and regularly worshiped at the Church of St. Mary Magdalene, or "Mary Mag's," as it was known in the university community. Similar views and a common experience opened the way naturally to a growing friendship.

Though Mark's path led him to the university and the life of a theologian, he always remained at heart a priest with a pastoral heart. Sundays and holy days found him preaching, teaching, and presiding in local congregations. Clergy and parishioners were deeply nourished by his warm and caring manner, and his ability to break the bread of the Word in such a gentle yet passionate way that made Scripture truly a word of life. "Mark is such a blessing," I would be told again and again not only by laypeople but also by clergy who saw in Mark a special quality: fidelity and prayerfulness knit together with an inquiring mind and a loving heart.

When I became presiding bishop of the Episcopal Church and Mark was a professor at Loyola University in Chicago, I asked him to serve as a chaplain to the bishops at their twice-a-year gatherings. His role was to preach at the daily Eucharist and to offer reflections in the course of the meeting. I wanted my Episcopal colleagues to have the experience of a theologian who was also a person of prayer. His words were manna in the midst of our institutional preoccupations, and a summons to reground ourselves in companionship with the Good Shepherd whose continuing ministry of care and oversight we had been ordained to share.

I also asked Mark to serve as Canon Theologian to the Presiding Bishop. I thought it was important for me to make plain the centrality of the theological enterprise to bishops. The ministry of a diocesan bishop is often fraught with administrative detail that, without intentional care, can overwhelm the deeper episcopal calling.

When Mark was diagnosed with ALS, my only thought was how I could express my love and caring and my gratitude for all that he has been and is in my life. I did not have to consider long, accepting with gratitude his invitation to offer reflections here and there in these two companion books. Our time spent working and reflecting together has been a huge gift to me. Any contribution I can make is for me one small way of saying, "Thank you, my most dear friend."

Frank T. Griswold

As We Begin

Perhaps you have observed, as I have, that many people — both those who are deeply connected to a Christian community and those who are not — are experiencing a deep hunger. Their hunger is a kind of *restlessness* (to borrow from Saint Augustine) that is seeking some transcendent focus: something that could enlarge our vision of life, deepen life's meaningfulness, clarify our self-understanding. Our seeking is of the Spirit, in that we are looking for something below the everyday surface of things that must be found and acknowledged for life to flourish.

We might look at our life as a garden in which plants, many and various, are growing, and we realize they need water. In the Gospel of John, Jesus speaks of a hidden spring of living water that is his to give, which assuages our thirst and helps us to grow into the person God is inviting us — through our restlessness — to become in grace and truth. Across the centuries, women and men have responded to this interior urgency in various ways. Among these has been the great common task

of helping each other to contemplate and understand more
deeply the mystery of God, who draws us toward divine life.

This divine friendship makes it possible for us to believe
and trust in God, to grow up into the fullness of God's meaning
for our lives and for our world — for God is infinite understanding as well as infinite love. God is always communicating and
teaching us, and this divine self-sharing — like seeds planted
at the heart of our lives — grows within us as a deepening spiritual life and as beliefs we share together, for God is "growing
us up" to share in God's own life. In fact, Jesus seems to think
of his own life and self-giving death as like a seed (John 12):
he plants himself deep within our lives so that the mystery of
God's life may bear much fruit within us for the sake of the
world he came to save.

To nurture and support each other as we grow in understanding our encounter with God in Christ, we try to put our
thoughts in words that we can share and talk about together.
So, when Christians have tried to explain in words what they
believe, they formulate Christian doctrines: the word "doctrine" derives from the Latin word for teaching. Each Christian belief finds some shared expression in the words of church
teachings, of theology, but these words are above all meant to
guide us toward the living mystery of God. In other words,
our faith reaches its fulfillment not in the words of theology
themselves but in the divine life toward which theology directs
us. It is my hope that exploring the central beliefs of Christian
faith together will allow their deep potential as seeds of faith,
as doorways to encounter, to become real for you.

Over the centuries, Christians have explored the richness of
church doctrines and have come to contemplate these shared
beliefs — whether about God's life as Trinity, or the incarnation
of God's Word as Jesus, or the pouring out of God's life within

us as grace — not as abstract and cerebral obfuscations making God more distant but as the all-enveloping force field in which we live and move and have our being. Theology, I believe, goes hand in hand with prayer: theology opens our hearts and minds to the vast wonder of what God is trying to teach us, and prayer draws us into transforming encounters with that inexhaustible goodness. Prayer, understood as our response to the indwelling Spirit and the alignment of our spirit with the life of the Trinity, takes us into the realm of divine mystery, which exceeds all we can ask or imagine, and which we experience as love.

It is my sense, informed over the decades, that nothing is more practical in taking us to this realm of divine mystery than mystical theology, for it holds theology and prayer together and leads us into the very heart of God's deep desire to communicate God's meaning, God's way of being, God's life with us. In the chapters that follow (as well as in the pages of the companion volume, *Harvest of Hope*), there are two central themes: the mystery of God, and the mystery of God's action to draw all beings into ever-closer relationship with God. But why do we call these things "mysteries," and what do we mean by the term "mystical theology"? The term "mystical" comes from the Greek verb meaning to close, as in to close the eyes: the mystical or a mystery is a reality more beautiful, more generous, more truthful than eyes can see or words express. Mystical theology attends to this inexpressibly wonderful dimension in every area of Christian faith. It always focuses on the hidden or mystical action of God in everything, and it always holds our beliefs open to God's own teaching — trusting God to draw us beyond our present understanding of these things and into God's own understanding of all things.

I suggest that mystical theology can help us recognize and respond to this divine communication that sets our lives ablaze with longing for eternity. It can be our means of attending to this restlessness, this tug, this pull, this fascination, this unsettlement, this yearning, this desire for something larger than ourselves. Mystical theology is about being real beyond our self-constructing: being real as God knows and loves us. In the First Letter of John we are told that "What we shall be has yet to be revealed." Mystical theology gives us the capacity for the personal and corporate appropriation of this dynamic of becoming, of entering into and being carried forward by our restlessness deeper into the mystery of God to discover who we truly are.

Christian teachings, contemplated in mystical theology, become true seeds of faith. For they help us to see that our journey through our mortal life is a rich symbol of an even greater journey — as we move from our limited mortal lives into our resurrection life, our sharing in God's endless love. C. S. Lewis speaks of these moments of awakening to eternity: "These things — the beauty, the memory of our own past — are good images of what we really desire; but if they are mistaken for the thing itself, they turn into dumb idols, breaking the hearts of their worshippers. For they are not the thing itself; they are only the scent of a flower we have not found, the echo of a tune we have not heard, news from a country we have never yet visited."*

This volume explores our fundamental Christian beliefs, and it is entitled *Seeds of Faith* because our Christian teachings are indeed like seeds: they plant within us "news from a country we have never yet visited." This good news helps us find our

---

* C. S. Lewis, "The Weight of Glory," in *The Weight of Glory and Other Addresses* (San Francisco: Harper Collins, 1949), 30–31.

way and uncovers within the depths of our mortal life a hidden or mystical fullness, a meaning that resonates within it and which Christian belief awakens us to hear — the meaning and voice of God who made us and loves us — from our life journey into our sharing in God's life by God's gift.

It is my deep sense that our common goal now, and our way forward, is to root and ground ourselves in the profound hope inherent in Christian belief. The theological virtue of hope is truly a precious gift as we taste and trust God's goodness, even when it seems absent. Hope transforms us as it makes us aware of our deepest desires and then offers them to God for our learning and our consolation. Mystical theology profoundly nourishes hope precisely because it explores the hidden and infinitely generous presence of God in all things. Mystical theology finds the hidden doorway from doctrine into prayer, from thinking about God to sharing in God's own thinking and loving of all things. It is our prayer that sharing in our conversations will help to lead you to this doorway.

The first set of chapters ponder the ways in which God awakens us to the divine presence, helping us to realize that Someone is addressing us and seeking our friendship. The middle chapters consider how God draws us into a deeper understanding of God's character and action in our world, above all in the life, death, and resurrection of Jesus Christ. And the later chapters in the book turn to the patterns of life that God the Holy Spirit weaves into our world — by helping us to become members of the body of Christ, the church, gracing us with deeper participation in Christ's relationship with the One who loves him, and thereby preparing us for the life to come and fellowship with all God's saints.

I hope this overview will serve as an invitation to join us in a journey of heart and mind and spirit into the realm of mystical theology, which is nothing less than an encounter with the One who, when asked his name by Moses, replied, "I AM WHO I AM" (Exod. 3:14).*

---

* Unless otherwise indicated, all scriptural quotations come from the New Revised Standard Version.

I

The Hidden Presence of God in All Things

Discovering Our Intimacy with God

Christians believe that God *is* love and is *in* love with all beings. God is the reason we — and our universe — exist, and is not simply another more powerful and invisible being alongside us within our world. What would happen if this belief came to life for us? Maybe a thought experiment could help us.

Imagine that we are all characters in a play; I don't mean that we are actors temporarily portraying the characters, but rather that we are the actual characters in a play. As such we have no notion that we *are* characters in a play; we simply see our present existence as what life is and that's it. It would never occur to us that there might be *another form of life*, of existence, of a mysteriously greater and deeper kind — the life of our author, our playwright.

Our analogy of God as author and we as characters suggests that at the very heart of every being is God's knowing of it. God is intimately present *within* every aspect of the world,

7

thinking and loving everything and everyone into existence moment by moment. God is wholly present within everything as an author is intimately present within everything in her book. Our author's thinking and loving sustain life moment by moment. Because God transcends the universe as its author, God is more intimately present *within* everything than another being alongside us could be. God's hidden or mystical presence within everything holds it in being.

Though we believe this, what would happen if it shaped our experience of our journey through life? Few things can help us grow more richly human than the abiding conviction that God loves us without reserve and will never turn away from us. We can always ask God for a sense of this intimate, loving, and life-giving presence in our lives. Most practices of meditation or awareness lead us to this understanding, as we allow ourselves to become aware: first, of the surface noise in our minds, and then of the passing play of thoughts and emotions — noticing all these with patience and compassion and then returning our focus to a deeper level of stillness, of awareness. In such moments of deeper awareness, we begin to sense the expansive radiance of God's intimately generous giving at the center of our beings, knowing and loving us in every moment.

Frank's Reflections on God's Authorship

I find myself pondering Mark's analogy of God as an author of a play or a novel in which we are expressions of the author's creativity. I note here that the word "author" comes from a Latin verb that means, among other things, "to originate," and therefore to "bring into being." That certainly is one of the classical ways in which we think about God — as the originator, the author of all things. I am aware too that Christ is described as an author in the Acts of the Apostles, in which Peter, in a speech to Jewish authorities, accuses them of having killed "the author of life." As well, when we reflect on the Trinity and proclaim the Word as the agent of creation, and then in the Nicene Creed refer to the Holy Spirit as the "giver of life," we immediately see that the originating and creating function is integral to the life of the Trinity. And in Wisdom of Solomon 13:3, God is proclaimed as the "author of beauty" reflected in creation.

From the word "author" we derive the word "authority," which instead of being defined as raw power can be thought of as the ability to impart life, that is, to bring things into being. Certainly, in this regard the authority of Jesus in the Gospels is one of bringing into fullness of being the blind and lame and those on the margins of society. When we speak of God or the persons of the Trinity bringing things into being, we recognize that we have been brought into being, and that we share from the moment of our creation in God's own life — in the way that an author's life and creative imagination bring characters into being. A human author decides what each character is going to do, the challenges each will face, and the resolution of various situations as they occur. However, in the case of God as an author, we have a loving parent who has given us the gift of free will and has chosen to imbue us with the capacity to love but allows us freedom to determine how that love is to be expressed: selfishly or selflessly. Just as loving parents do not want a child looking endlessly at them for an indication of what to do, so God allows us a full range of possibilities, as did

the father of the prodigal son, in the hope that the choices we
make, and what we discover along the way through trial and
error, will lead us ever more into a fullness of selfhood that is
God's deepest desire for us.

If one stays with the analogy of God as author of a play or
a novel, it is worth pointing out that human authors often are
surprised to discover that, in the course of delineating their
characters, their characters break free and say or do things that
come as a surprise. Many an author has said at the end of a
book: "I had no idea that it would end this way. It certainly
wasn't in my original plot outline." For example, Madeleine
L'Engle, in her book *Walking on Water*, relates how she was surprised by the actions of characters she herself had created.

As I meet this analogy in the course of Mark's rich and
engaging reflections, I remind myself that the divine author
has created us to share God's life and to express that life in love
that is free and ever unfolding.

Why Analogies Are Helpful in Theology

I find myself wanting to reflect on *why* I am drawn to this
analogy between authors and their novels, and God and the
universe. We will return to it a number of times throughout
this book (and in our companion volume), and so its strengths
and weaknesses as an analogy are worth pondering. Frank's
reflections just above not only help us to think more deeply
about authorship but also help us to recognize an important
disadvantage to the authorial analogy. Even though human authors are sometimes startled by the unexpected vivacity of their
characters, as Frank reminds us, still, we normally do think of

everything within the world of a novel as fixed and determined by the author's creative intention: nothing within the world of the novel normally gets to make its own decisions!

So, we need to think, as Frank does, about how God's authoring of us, unlike the authoring of a human artist, is the very *source* of our human freedom rather than its denial. Human authors, no matter how wonderfully inventive they may be, have a finite imagination, and their characters are tethered by that; but God's loving imagination is infinite and inexhaustibly creative. God gives us *ourselves* moment by moment, with the freedom to discover the authentic truth of that gift and live into it.

There are other aspects of the authorial analogy, however, that have become deeply helpful to me — and I hope they will be for you as well. I'm writing these words using dictation software because, as we noted earlier in the book, I am living in the later stages of ALS. My body is now paralyzed except, blessedly, for the ability to speak and to swallow — though my speech is beginning to be impaired. Much of who I am seems to be falling away from me and into silence. I have been immensely helped during this season by pondering the Christian belief that the deepest truth of who I am is not buried within me and subject to my own physical diminishment and death; rather, my identity is sustained within God's friendship with me, and the reality of my life flows from God's everlasting knowing and loving of me. And of God's knowing and loving of us, there is no end.

But why does theology even use this kind of thinking by way of *analogy*, this analogical imagination? Why use analogies to talk about our life and God's? Because there are wonders in the life of God we cannot comprehend. And so a good analogy can help us to start our journey toward understanding: by allowing us to think about the things we do know, a good analogy allows us to use those things to move in the right direction toward the things we cannot yet understand. For example, we cannot look directly at the sun without blinding ourselves, but we can "see" the sun by observing the beauty it brings to light as it shines on the world around us. The bright shining beauty that radiates through a sunlit maple leaf gives us a way of imagining the source of that brightness, namely, the sun itself. Analogies help us to reach across from what we *can* understand to what we cannot yet comprehend. They are crucial to the work of theology precisely because theology is the work of faith seeking greater understanding; it is the life that hopes in what is still unseen.

Fortunately, Christians believe, God has created a universe that is *inherently* analogical, symbolic, sacramental. For every good and perfect thing that we can know in our universe receives its existence, its goodness, from God, who *is* Existence and Goodness. Because of this, our world, at least in all that is good and true and beautiful, points toward the Source of that goodness, truth, and beauty — who is God. And that means that the world is, as I said above, inherently analogical, inherently pointing from the things that we can see to their full plenitude and source in God, the Author of all things.

Four Ways of Recognizing God in Our Lives

Let me briefly summarize the four ways in which the authorial analogy has helped me, and then I can explain them a little more fully. First, the analogy helps me to think about the very fact that we need analogies! In other words, it helps me to think about the *difference* between our kind of existence and the fullness of life who is God. Second, the analogy helps me to ponder and appreciate the great *intimacy* of God's hidden or mystical presence at the heart of everything. Third, it helps me to think more deeply about *how* God is present — about how it is the very *pattern and rhythm of God's own life* that touch and infuse our lives. And fourth, it helps me to recognize *our deep common kinship with all other beings,* for we all flow forth into time from the everlasting unity and communion of God.

Consider, then, the first way in which our authorial analogy can help us. When we talk about our life and God's life, we are easily misled by the fact that we use the same word, "life," to refer to both kinds of existence! But the authorial analogy helps us to remember that our finite existence is but a reflection into time and space of an infinitely greater kind of existence — just as the existence of characters in a novel is a reflection of their author's life and depends upon that life. While this analogy helps us remember the mysterious "beyondness" or transcendence of God, it also helps us recognize the reflection of God in all beings. The beauty of every seashell, the goodness of every just act, the joy of every child's laughter are all expressions in time and space of the infinite beauty, goodness, and joy that are the very life of God. But are we destined only to hear rumors of God's great goodness in the world around us but never to share in it ourselves? Could characters in a novel ever "journey" beyond the world of the novel to share in the life of their author?

Astonishingly, God seems to be so in love with all creatures that God desires to bring them from their finite experience of all that is wonderful into the very source of that wonder, the inexhaustible wonder of God's own life. The world and the life that we know now turn out to be only the beginning of our adventure. Christian mystical theology contemplates how God lovingly brings us from our mortal existence into communion with the everlasting life of God. This infinite passing over would indeed be as if an author could bring one of the characters from her novel into the real world of her own life. Perhaps we could imagine her doing this by awakening her character's awareness of her hidden presence within the character's present form of life — and the character's desire to share in her greater life. And in fact this is what Jesus and the Holy Spirit do — awaken us to a mysterious destiny written in our very hearts, which ever calls us beyond ourselves and into the life of God.

This leads us to the second reason why I find the authorial analogy so helpful. Because it gives us a way of thinking about *how* God *is* present to us and with us. God, as we said above, is not another being within our world who stands apart from us or tries somehow to get close to us. Like authors who are present by their creative artistry and delight at the heart of everything in their novels, God is intimately present at the heart of all creatures — always understanding and loving them into being. Every thought I think, every word I speak, is an act of God. Not because God takes my place or forces me to do anything, but rather because moment by moment God is at the very core of my being, giving me myself, calling me toward the fullness of who I might become.

And this suggests a third way in which the authorial analogy can help us — giving us a window into the *manner* of God's presence. Think of how a really great author enjoys a profound self-awareness or self-understanding. We could even say that this is the precondition for his artistry. For he is able to bring forth from the deep meaning of his experience just the right ideas that can inform and give life to the characters in his novel. In other words, the creative imagination at the heart of the characters is nothing less than the deep word or meaning of the author's own life.

In an analogous way, Christians believe, God eternally contemplates Godself and in doing so brings forth the Word who is the full meaning and understanding of all that God is. It is this eternal Word who speaks at the heart of every creature, speaks just the right idea of God's own life that gives us ourselves, our own unique way of being in time. For what the analogy especially helps us to see is that God's Word, God's thinking at the heart of each of us, is nothing less than God's thinking and understanding of Godself. And that is why we exist as the beloved reflections within time of different aspects of God's infinite life.

But authors not only bring forth the word or meaning of their own life, by which they give vitality to their characters. They also embrace and affirm that truth of themselves that becomes resonant as the heart of their characters. They rejoice and love to see this reality unfold in all its possibilities within the world of their novels. This offers us an analogy to the coming forth of God's own joy and love, God the Holy Spirit: for God not only eternally brings forth the Word who is the very meaning and truth of God, but God also affirms and delights in that truth — and this inexhaustible love and delight Christians call God the Holy Spirit. So our analogy helps us to see that God's infinite delight in each creature is nothing less than the eternal joy and love of God for God. In other words, the love by which God loves each one of us is the very same eternal love of God's own life, the love of God for God's own goodness and truth.

The historical presence of Jesus and the Holy Spirit at work in our world, as "characters" within our world, turns out to be how God restores our consciousness of God's authoring intimacy within us — and within all beings. The Christian mystical journey follows the path of this awakening consciousness, the consciousness of God thinking and loving all beings into existence. And that is the fourth reason why the authorial analogy speaks to me, because it helps me to ponder how I might become more attentive and attuned to God's meaning and desire, God's Word and God's Spirit, at the heart of all things. Attending to God in this way has helped me not only to live into the truth of myself, as a continuous gift of God, but also to realize more deeply that we are *all* coming forth from God's eternal knowing and loving — that in the mind and heart of God we are *united*, we flow forth from that divine unity. Our differences can never be the reason for divisions, for our kinship and unity as fellow creatures are the deepest and truest dimension of us.

Learning How God Communicates with Us

In the chapters that follow, we will explore many ways in which God's hidden or mystical presence in all beings comes to light across the great symphony of Christian beliefs — and helps us glimpse the hope we share for life together in God. Over many years of talking with people about their spiritual life, about how God seems to them, I have come to believe that God gives each of us a number of particularly significant moments, moments when God opens our minds and hearts to God's meaning and love in our life. Often these moments are buried in our past, and asking God to help us recall them (and to help us understand more of what God wants to teach us through them) can be wonderfully helpful. In the hope of encouraging you to search through your own memories with God's help, I might describe a moment of such grace from my own life.

When I was growing up, among my dearest and closest friends was our family's dog, a golden retriever named Chiz. He was, to my childhood self, enormous and powerful, yet his fur was the softest thing I knew. To rest your head on his side was to curl up within a blazing sunset, and to look into his deep brown eyes was to know yourself loved without limit. When I look back on our adventures in the neighborhood together, I sense that God gave me such a wonderful companion so that I might more easily awaken to God's beauty and love all around me.

One summer, when I was old enough to cross the road, Chiz and I began the exploration of a vacant lot nearby. I know now that it could not have been nearly as vast a region as I experienced it then, but at the time it was clearly an enchanted land whose farthest reaches might remain unknown forever. Its outer flanks were fiercely guarded by thickets of buckthorn, and I was certain that only Chiz could have found us a path inside. He charged through the sumac and hickory trees. His exuberance taught me to delight in wonders I might never have seen for myself, except through his eyes. And sometimes we would rest for a while beneath an oak, its upper branches singing a wind song whose words I could never quite make out — though it seemed, by his discerning sniffing of the air, that Chiz might somehow know its meaning. I realize now that this beloved dog was the guide and teacher who helped me experience the real enchantment, the deeper magic at the heart of things, that in later years I recognized as God's love and wisdom.

That golden summer seemed as if it might stretch onward forever, but soon summer turned into fall, year followed year. And as we each grew older at our different paces, I could see that my friend's kind and noble muzzle was growing ever whiter. When he died, I was inconsolable, and certainly the love he showed me and I showed him helped me begin to conceive how deep and vast love might be. And more than that, our friendship taught me that love is itself a form of knowing, a way of reaching into the heart of things and recognizing something wonderful and precious.

One windswept, cloud-scudding autumn day several months after Chiz died, I wandered back to the vacant lot that had been our enchanted woods. His absence was numbing to me, and I could feel that the magic of the place had drained away with him. I poked my way aimlessly through old haunts of ours, missing desperately my dear friend's exhilaration at each new smell, each new trace of something just beyond our reach. Then through a thicket of wild roses I saw what seemed to be a clearing in the woods I didn't remember being there.

I knew that Chiz would never have hesitated to push through into the opening, so I followed his inspiration and found myself in an open space filled with fragrant grass and a young maple tree. Suddenly the leaden sky broke open and sunlight showered into the clearing. The leaves of the maple tree changed instantly from a dull ocher to brilliant gold and crimson, each leaf rippling in the wind and blazing brightness into the world. In that moment I had a sense of immense and limitless goodness, of joy beyond words.

Over the years I have held out these memories to God in prayer many times, for I sensed that deeply woven through them all was God's meaning and God's love, unlimited resource. As I said above, I deeply believe that we all have such seasons when God teaches us our own language, the vocabulary of our unique conversation with God. For me, this language has communicated many of the insights that the authorial analogy conveys. Part of what I have heard when I have prayed over that one amazing, brilliant autumn day, was that the bright exhilaration and flashing joy, which reminded me so much of my beloved childhood companion, was indeed a sign of all the goodness and friendship we had shared — because it was a sign of the One who *gave* us our friendship, and who by that very means began to wake me up to the bright immensity of joy who is God.

Love and loss, beauty beyond possession, have all pointed me toward an infinite goodness from which our present experience of goodness comes. And though the wonders and enchantments of our present life are limited and mortal, they are nonetheless — or can be if we learn from them — a bridge God throws across infinity, for at the heart of all the good we have known and yet must lose has been the love of God's own life, beckoning us onward — where all that is lost is found, and all that has died yet lives in fullness everlasting. For nothing can be lost in the mind and heart of our Maker.

We hope that these reflections on the mystical presence of God in our earthly life, and how God awakens us to that presence in order to draw us into God's everlasting life, will encourage and guide you in the chapters ahead. In our companion volume, *Harvest of Hope: A Contemplative Approach to Holy Scripture*, you will find the seeds, the ideas, we have considered in this volume growing and bearing fruit in our meditation on the Scriptures for the church year.

Faith and Fear

Faith as God's Friendship

When people think about their faith, sometimes they feel uneasy about experiences of doubt or uncertainty. But in fact, the antagonist of faith is not doubt but fear. Faith is what grows within us as we become more aware of God's deep love and desire for friendship with us. In any friendship, sometimes we just don't understand our friend, and sometimes we can't see how what our friend tells us can be true. That doesn't undermine our friendship, however; but what does work against it is fear — fear that maybe our friend doesn't care about us as much as we thought, or fear that deep down we aren't really lovable. At its heart, then, faith is what grows within us as God awakens us to God's inexhaustible love for us — a love that will never turn away from us, a love that sets us free from fear.

An analogy in the last chapter suggested that our relationship as creatures to God is like that of characters within a play or a novel to their author. This analogy helps us to see that there is a wonderful but hard-to-recognize difference between our kind of existence and that of our author. If you were a character in a play, how could you even begin to imagine that your existence flows continually from the creative life of your author? And yet, because God desires to share divine life with us, we do need some way of learning about that life and moving toward it. This is what faith is: our way of hearing what God is teaching us, and trusting God enough to keep moving toward a deeper understanding.

The Letter to the Hebrews helps us imagine the transcendent promise of life with God by thinking about the journey of Abraham and all his descendants. The letter poignantly emphasizes that even though Abraham and his people did spend time in the promised land, their faith (God's friendship with them) kept them open and longing for a yet more unimaginable fulfillment, for a different kind of homeland:

By faith Abraham obeyed when he was called to set out for a place that he was to receive as an inheritance; and he set out, not knowing where he was going. By faith he stayed for a time in the land he had been promised, as in a foreign land, living in tents. . . . For he looked forward to the city that has foundations, whose architect and builder is God. . . . All of these [descendants of Abraham] died in faith without having received the promises, but from a distance they saw and greeted them. They confessed that they were strangers and foreigners on the earth, for people who speak in this way make it clear that they are seeking a homeland. If they had been thinking of the land that they had left behind, they would have had opportunity to return. But as it is, they desire a better country, that

is, a heavenly one. Therefore God is not ashamed to be
called their God; indeed, he has prepared a city for them.
(Heb. 11:8–16)

The faith of Abraham and his children allowed them to
journey through time and space in a way that kept them open
and hoping for a reality beyond time and space, a city "whose
architect and builder is God." Their friendship with God created within them a profound awareness that their true fulfillment could never be something "that they had left behind," for
by faith they came to "desire a better country, that is, a heavenly one." This passage is deeply moving because it speaks of
the stunning awareness that must have dawned upon Abraham
and his people: even though they had finally arrived in the land
of promise, their friendship with God made them realize that
the promised land itself was a sign of an infinitely greater reality.

How God Draws Us toward God's Own Life

By befriending us and giving us faith, God allows us to glimpse
and touch a reality we cannot yet fully comprehend. Our faith
can reach even through what seems to us to be the barrier of
death, allowing us to catch sight of and touch the promise of
our life in God. For this reason, the Letter to the Hebrews describes faith as "the assurance of things hoped for, the conviction of things not seen" (Heb. 11:1). Because God loves us,
God imbues us with this assurance or conviction, this taste
and touch, of a life that is really Life itself. But how does faith
actually help us move toward this fulfillment we can barely
dream of? How can it tell us of our heavenly homeland in a way

that, on the one hand, we can make some sense of but that, on the other hand, does not let us shrink the divine reality to our present way of thinking?

Returning to our analogy might help us ponder these questions. How could an author help her characters journey from their life within the world of her novel into the world of her greater life as their author? How could an author communicate with her characters, in a way they could understand, but also in a way that would awaken them to a reality they could *not* yet see? For an author to do this, she would have to write characters into the world of her novel who could begin to open the minds and hearts of the other characters to this unbelievable possibility — that there *is* a greater world, and a greater kind of life to which they might belong.

Something like this is pretty much what Christians believe has happened through the story of Israel and Christ. God sends prophets and poets, visionaries and leaders, and even God's very own meaning as the author of all things, God's Word made flesh (Jesus), into our world of creatures. These messengers from our author awaken within us an awareness (faith) that there is a greater world, the world of our author, and that God desires us to share in that greater life from which we flow. So, the beliefs of Christian faith use the imagery and concepts of *this* world to open us toward the world of *God*, the life of God. By telling us of the journey to the promised land, God helps us to imagine and to believe in life itself as a journey into communion with God.

This infinite leap from being creatures to being creatures-who-share-in-God's-life is not something we could ever achieve for ourselves. God just gives it to us because God is in love with us and created us to share in this greater life. The wonderful mystery of our existence as human beings is that we have been created for a life beyond our own kind of life. Thus, God's friendship with us begins to imbue our present lives with the characteristics and virtues that can move us toward our life to come, our life in God's Life. We call these the theological virtues because they help us imagine and live into our divine life: faith, hope, and love.

We might imagine each of these virtues as God's life, God's friendship, at work within us, deepening and strengthening and extending the very best aspects of who we each are — so that we blossom into the fullness of who God has always known and loved us to be. In a sense, faith comes first among the theological virtues because we could not hope for or love a reality we have not heard about. But hope and love sustain and guide faith, keeping it open toward a fullness that, in our present life, we cannot fully know. Love and hope are so crucial to faith because without them our faith could unwittingly shrink the promises of God to what we can grasp within our present knowledge. And so, love and hope nurture and guide our faith; they will not let it rest content with anything less than the full goodness and beauty of God.

The What, How, *and* Why *of Faith*

As we talk with God and fellow Christians about faith, it can be helpful to think about faith in three dimensions — each of which can be pondered with relish and great spiritual fruitfulness. We can remember these as the *what*, the *how*, and the *why* of faith. The first aspect is *what* God is teaching us, through the church's reading of Scripture, through worship, and through all the moments of our life. Our shared faith, expressed in the creeds, offers us a rich itinerary for prayer. For every statement of our belief opens onto the endless wonder and mystery of its reality in God. You might, for example, read the story of Jesus teaching his friends through a parable, and then ask the Holy Spirit to awaken you to Christ's inward teaching in your own life. What might God long to help you understand? What do you wish the Spirit might unfold within you?

The second aspect of faith is *how* we hold these beliefs as true — even though we cannot yet fully understand them. Just as the light of the sun is how we can see the reality and beauty of the world around us, so the infinite light of God's own knowing and loving allows us to think about the beliefs of faith. God's power of knowing is how we begin to understand what God is teaching us, because in faith God gives us a share of God's own understanding of all things. Think of how the knowledge of a really good friend can help you think about something you yourself don't fully understand. We can always ask God to illumine our hearts more deeply and set us free from any fears that make it harder for us to share in God's own knowing of all things. We might ask Christ to help us practice this, perhaps by sharing with us his own experience of learning and growing within the love of the One who sent him.

And the third aspect of faith is *why* we believe. We believe because God awakens within us the love and hope that keep faith strong and open to the genuine fullness of God. Suppose we were in the most beautiful of gardens but had no desire to see what's around us and no expectation of being amazed. Then, the reality and beauty of our surroundings would say nothing to us. In a far deeper sense, the love and hope that God pours out within us arouse our faith to keep us moving into the wonders of God's teaching. We can always ask God to give us more love and more hope; there is nothing God would rather give us! Sometimes there are deep and unrecognized hurts that make it hard for us to receive the love and hope God longs to give us; asking God to help us understand these and to heal us can be a life-giving step.

In my experience, talking about faith with people can often surface some negative feelings that may have become impediments to spiritual growth. For instance, some people might feel they have not always been very faithful and consequently would rather avoid talking about faith. Or others may have been exposed to a very rigid and oppressive form of faith and been hurt by the very thing that ought to have given them life. Giving people permission to talk about these experiences helps make it possible to explore the more positive spiritual significance of faith. As our sense of God's love for us deepens, it becomes much more natural for us to grow in faith. We can begin to see that accepting the beliefs of Christianity neither oppresses our sense of self nor arrives at the goal by clinging inflexibly to certain words or ways of thought. Frank helps us think more deeply about this question of the personal appropriation of faith in what he says below.

Frank's Reflections on Faith and Fear

I believe God loves me, but that is in my mind. I accept the fact that God loves me, but how does that become more than a mental abstraction but rather real, as something I both know

and feel? Here I think once again of Saint Augustine saying that we are restless until we rest in God. I have given space within myself to the fact that God loves me. Faith is the work of the Spirit within me. But the invitation does not stop there. I am in the doorway of something larger and deeper. It is like saying "I believe in God" the way I believe the tree I see on the corner is actually there. But this doesn't change me. So, faith is God's gift and an open invitation to more — rather than an end in itself. We are given the yearning and the restlessness and the sense that there is more that the Spirit works within us "with sighs too deep for words."

Faith, as Mark has observed, can be countered by fear that I am not lovable. So, to know and feel that God loves me may be impeded experientially because of an interior accusing voice that is only too happy to point out my deficiencies, my limitations, my hypocrisies, my sins — which thereby render me unlovable in my own eyes. I think here of Peter encountered by Jesus, the embodiment of love, and crying out, "Depart from me, for I am a sinful man." This sense of being unworthy can be reinforced by placing greater emphasis on "Christ died for my sins" than on "Christ rose from the dead" — and I too through baptism am invited to rise with him as he draws all people to himself and reminds us that he came to give us life and give it abundantly.

The interior judging voice is one of the classic guises adopted by Satan — a name that simply means accuser or adversary. Or, to borrow from Saint Paul: it is an instance of Satan masquerading as an angel of light. Jesus reveals God's love for us, and the Holy Spirit weaves the divine love into the fabric of our personal depths. And yet this interior voice counterposed to God's love is very seductive: it seems virtuous and humble to focus on our shortcomings and failures — such that we arm ourselves against the larger truth of God's love through resistance and self-judgment.

The seventeenth-century priest-poet George Herbert wonderfully captures this classic struggle within us — as faith draws us more deeply from believing with the mind to experiencing in the depths of our hearts that we are loved by God.

"Love (III)"

> Love bade me welcome, yet my soul drew back,
>> Guilty of dust and sin.
> But quick-ey'd Love, observing me grow slack
>> From my first entrance in,
> Drew nearer to me, sweetly questioning
>> If I lack'd any thing.
>
> "A guest," I answer'd, "worthy to be here";
>> Love said, "You shall be he."
> "I, the unkind, ungrateful? ah my dear,
>> I cannot look on thee."
> Love took my hand, and smiling did reply,
>> "Who made the eyes but I?"
>
> "Truth, Lord, but I have marr'd them; let
>> my shame
>> Go where it doth deserve."
> "And know you not," says Love, "who bore
>> the blame?"

"My dear, then I will serve."

"You must sit down," says Love, "and taste

my meat."

So I did sit and eat.

Faith Always Goes in Search of Understanding

We could say that the life of faith is a life of ongoing growth and conversion. Faith is always searching for deeper understanding, because our love for our divine friend moves us to long for a clearer vision of God's truth. Sometimes people speak of faith as a "leap in the dark." And it is certainly true that the brightness and overwhelming reality of what God longs to share with us in faith can dazzle and overwhelm us — as when a friend who understands something wonderfully and intricately beautiful tries to help us catch a glimpse of this reality, even though at the time it's more than we can fully grasp. I well remember the time a dear nephew of mine who is a physicist tried to explain quantum mechanics to me! Though I was pretty well lost in the overwhelming reality he was trying to explain, nevertheless, because of my affection for him and trust in him, I was able, for a while at least, to glimpse something of what he was telling me.

Thus, healthy Christian belief is never the undoing or rejection of our understanding. For faith is always an act of our minds being drawn by God toward the life-giving truth that alone can fulfill our minds — the truth who is God. And this is what, Christians believe, God ultimately longs to give us: such a sharing in God's life of communion, of self-giving knowing and loving, that we come to know God no longer by faith but by sharing in God's own knowing and loving of Godself. Then faith or belief will no longer be necessary because we will see and know the truth of God, and taste and rejoice in the goodness of God. And of this, Christians believe, there will be no end, because God is *infinite* goodness, truth, and beauty.

Revelation

How Not *to Hear God*

To think that the source of the universe desires to befriend us can be wonderfully overwhelming. To recall our analogy, it would be as if we were characters within the world of a novel who gradually came to realize that the life and meaning at the heart of ourselves and of everything in our world was trying to communicate with us. At first we would inevitably think that this voice, this presence, was simply another being within our world, more powerful than us perhaps, but otherwise more or less like us. No doubt we would connect this voice with particularly prominent features of our world — it would be the voice of a sacred mountain, or of the sun perhaps, or of a legendary ancestor. We would, in other words, think of this powerful presence as what ancient people called a "god."

In a similar way, scholars tell us, the ancient tribes (who would eventually become united as the people of Israel) each related to their own tribal god as pretty much like all the other gods they heard about— except that *this* god happened to be the local deity of *their* land. Everyone knew how things worked between human beings and their gods: you would try to figure out what pleased your deity and make offerings to it in the hope that it would favor you with a good harvest or more male children or a satisfying revenge upon your enemies. The more powerful groups of people could make more splendid sacrifices, and so they always seemed to get the more powerful gods on their side.

God's self-communication to Israel began the long and difficult spiritual conversion that liberated Israel from what we might think of as humankind's natural religion: your god powerfully reinforces your identity and confirms your views and prejudices against people who are different from you, who are so clearly *not* favored by God. Everyone knew that if you are doing well in life, that means God favors you, and if you are poor or suffering or of another race or diseased, then you must be degenerate and have done bad things that cause God to punish you. And, of course, all the gods demand sacrifices if you want their favor, and while it is usually more expedient to sacrifice people who are not like you, quite often it seems that the god demands that you or your children or your society should be or act or think a certain way if you want to be accepted and loved by the god. Sometimes this means that you have to sacrifice some dimension of your own life (perhaps your honesty about who you really are, or perhaps your firstborn child). And if bad things happen to you, you have clearly deserved what you get as a punishment from the gods.

God Reveals Who God Really Is

I exaggerate all this in order to help us recognize how appalling this natural yet damaged perception actually is. Yet there are many outspoken Christians whose belief continues to be shadowed by these impulses. In fact, apart from the grace of the true and living God, most of us would likely believe this way for the simple reason that it accords with the natural course of things: the powerful do what they will and the weak suffer what they must (and apparently deserve to), and the gods legitimize and thrive upon this order grounded in power, envy, violence, and fear. God reveals Godself, at least in part, *in order to set humankind free from this distorted experience of reality,* thus beginning the long and sometimes painful process of liberating us from the idols that dominate and oppress us.

Over many centuries Israel began to notice things about its god that seemed unlike the other gods, even though Israel could not always fully understand the significance of these things. For example, in the old tribal stories in Genesis, Israel's god seemed very strangely to favor *not* the older and more powerful brother (as would only be natural) but always the younger and weaker one. In fact, contrary to all natural religious wisdom, Israel's god claimed to have chosen Israel *not* because it was more numerous or more powerful – in fact, at the time Israel was reduced to slavery in Egypt – but simply because God loved Israel.

In later centuries Israel was again in exile, having suffered defeat by more powerful peoples, whose gods were presumably much more powerful than Israel's god. But then Israel's god stirred up other nations and used them to achieve Israel's freedom and return home – as though somehow Israel's god had authority far beyond Israel itself. And during this time Israel's sages and priests and prophets pondered these things about their god and began to understand their meaning. It seemed to them that perhaps, almost beyond human comprehension, their god was far more powerful than the other gods — yet not by means of the power of violence. One of the priests tried to understand how this could be, how the power of God could be unlike the power of one being in competition with another, but more like the power of love within everything, the power that helps all beings to become alive, to become themselves. To imagine this, he wrote a new beginning to the book of Genesis, suggesting that Israel's god is the one reality who is *not* part of the world of conflicting powers and rivalries at all, but is rather the creator of heaven and earth, the author of all things. In a sly critique of the Babylonian creation stories, the author of the prologue to Genesis portrays God as creating not by means of a violent conquest of rival gods but simply by calling all things into existence through an act of free, intelligent, and loving speech — as a singer calls his song into being.

Over centuries God patiently and lovingly drew Israel into friendship, and through that relationship, Israel gradually became more and more able to receive the deep truth about God that God longs to pour out within human hearts. Think of how a wonderful and long-standing friendship reveals the realities of friends to each other. We are changed by such friendships; sometimes it seems as if the life of a friend becomes a living word to us that opens our own eyes and shapes our own way of being.

And so, Christians believe, it was and is for us: the God of Israel reveals a mysterious depth of wisdom and love that grows within our lives like a Word of meaning whose significance opens our eyes to everything and changes how we act. God speaks the deep truth of God's own life as a Word who becomes flesh within our lives and helps us to know and name God, not by giving us new or better information about God, but by befriending us and drawing us into God's own knowing and loving of Godself, filling us with God's meaning or Word and God's joy or Spirit.

Jesus's friends seem to have been drawn to him because he understood them so profoundly and accepted them in a way that changed their lives. And at the same time, this very process of being known and loved by Jesus seemed to include being invited by him into his own relationship with the one he called Father. In fact, Christians came to believe that Jesus's relationship to the Father is the expression in our world of God's infinite act of self-understanding and self-communication. God's life, in other words, includes this perfect and beautiful communication of infinite truth, and we call this eternal self-communication the coming forth of the eternal Word in God — the Word whom we believe is incarnate as Jesus Christ. Saint Thomas Aquinas puts it like this: "Since God by understanding himself understands all other things, . . . the Word conceived in God by his understanding of himself must also be the Word of all things."* Thus, revelation is always an encounter with the Word, who draws us into God's self-understanding and also therefore into the understanding, the Word, of all things. Revelation is our meeting with the One who understands us from within, as only our author can, and who also understands and cherishes *all* beings.

How God's Self-Revealing Friendship Transforms Us

And what does this all mean for us in our own lives today? We believe as Christians that God is always communicating

---

* Thomas Aquinas, *Summa contra gentiles* 4.13.6, trans. Charles J. O'Neil (Notre Dame, IN: University of Notre Dame Press, 1975), 94.

Godself to us and within us — because it is the very nature of God to share God's life. And yet it is probably true for most of us that, in a variety of ways, the brokenness of our world has shadowed and distorted our experience of God. We may carry within us, perhaps without realizing it, a sense that God is untrustworthy or punitive or harshly judgmental, or likely to demand something terrible of us. The story of Israel's liberation from such images of God can be a starting point for talking with people about how God seems to them. Very often it turns out that no one has ever asked them about this or invited them to notice and acknowledge their most genuine feelings about God — and doing so will certainly need to be accompanied by prayer that the Holy Spirit will guide and strengthen their inner discernment.

Sometimes a person feels a simple kind of numbness with regard to God, or a silent absence that may well be attended by spiritual dryness and the sense that prayer is a waste of time and perhaps uncomfortable. These are perfectly natural reactions within our human spirit to the impressions of the harsh or angry punitive gods that our upbringing may have imposed on us. Confronted with such idols, one would quite understandably want to keep well away from God! Again, helping people frame their sense of God by the story of God's rescuing revelation of Godself may be an important source of clarity and consolation.

It may help to understand this process of inner conversion and liberation to liken it to the experience of growing up. As children, we formed our world around the things that were most powerful for us: the things we feared, the things we most prized, the things that made us happy. In the ancient world these things would have been gods to us. And when from time to time a parent or teacher intruded upon our world, suggesting that there might be other things that would become even more important to us, this was experienced as a kind of threat — or at least an interruption in our world. Though we could not understand it at the time, the world of our childhood could not fulfill us and would stunt us if we tried to remain there. We may not have understood *why* we should learn to read or try new kinds of food or make new friends from other places. The process of doing these things often felt as though we were being pried away from the world we knew and had settled into, for all its goods and evils. In a much deeper way, God's self-revelation breaks into the world we have settled into and begins the slow but ultimately joyful process of growing us into the wider reality of God's world, the world of God's truth and love, the world in which we can at last grow into the truth of ourselves as God has always known and loved us.

Finding God in All Things

Christians believe that the whole creation, including our own stories, as well as the wisdom and writings of all peoples, is God's *general revelation* — by the fact that all things *exist*, only and always, because God is communicating Godself within them as the gift of their very existence. The *special revelation* of the biblical witness to God's action in Israel and Christ is meant to help us interpret God's meaning in everything — including our own lives. Thus, talking with people about revelation should help and encourage them to find God in all things. Praying the Scriptures allows God to help us recognize the divine life at work all around us.

As we read the Scriptures and listen for God speaking to us, we can also contemplate the wonders of each blade of grass, every tiny child, every struggle for justice — and ask God to help us hear the divine meaning in all things. The mystery of revelation awakens us to the One who is always and in all things longing to share life with us, and whose meaning is always love.

Frank's Reflections on Revelation

If we believe Saint Paul when he states that through baptism we become limbs and members of Christ's risen body, the church, and that the Holy Spirit — the Spirit of the Son — dwells within us, we then become bearers of the Word to one another. With this in mind, I was struck by Mark's reflections upon the re-velatory nature of friendship, and that friendship reveals the reality of friends to one another. That is, I am revealed to my-self through the loving and truth-bearing gaze of an intimate other, and, at the same time, my friend is more fully known to himself through my returning gaze of love and truth. I note here that in his treatise *On Spiritual Friendship*, Aelred extols the benefits of friendship as a stage in our knowing and loving God and becoming God's friend.

Intimate friendships, in which we feel secure and loved, allow us to reveal ourselves, to set aside our defenses and take off our masks. And, in this openness to our friend, we make it possible to be known by another in ways we may not know our-selves. Such deep friendship, rooted in the shared love poured into our hearts by the Holy Spirit, allows Christ the Word to "speak" through words from a friend: words of insight, encouragement, compassion, forgiveness, painful truth — such that we grow in grace and truth as Christ advances "his full shape in us" not as we might wish, but according to Christ's paschal pattern of dying and rising and making all things (including each one of us) new. As Mark reminds us, "Revelation is our meeting with the One who understands us from within." Such is the nature of what Julian of Norwich calls the "royal friendship" of Christ, that the true self has to be delivered from the various self-constructions in which we find our security and identity, in order to enter into the freedom for which Christ, "the author of life," has set us free.

All this reminds us that revelation can be profoundly intimate and personal and close at hand. It can be conveyed by a word, a look, a silence; it can be clothed in something so ordinary or seemingly "inappropriate" in relation to our sensibilities, that without a discerning eye, it may pass us by. Here I am reminded of God's address to Moses, "The word is very near you; it is in your mouth and in your heart for you to observe" (Deut. 30:14). The word, God's self-disclosing speech, is Christ, the Word, who still has many things to say, but we cannot bear them now (John 16:12). Revelation, therefore, continues to unfold as the Spirit draws from the "boundless riches of Christ" (Eph. 3:8), and with a love that passes all understanding, makes "many things" heard and known in the depths of our hearts. "O that today," cries the psalmist, "you would listen to his voice!" (Ps. 95:7).

4

The Mystery of the Trinity

God as Infinite Self-Giving

Our faith in God as Trinity grows directly from our experience of salvation, of being reconciled to God in Christ by the power of his Spirit. Christians have found themselves drawn by the Holy Spirit into Christ's relationship with the One he called Father, and so we have been led to say that our God is a communion of infinitely self-giving wisdom and love, the Trinity. In what follows, I will describe how Christians came to enter into the life of this great mystery of God as the Trinity of Father, Son, and Holy Spirit.

In the years after the death and resurrection of Jesus, his closest followers found themselves transformed in ways they could barely begin to understand. The risen Christ poured out within them forgiveness, love, and a powerful sense of his joyful boldness, his Spirit. In his presence, they began to reinterpret their Scriptures (as we see happening in Luke's story of the walk to Emmaus).

It seemed to his friends that, throughout his ministry, Jesus had continually embraced whatever or whomever he met — insufficient loaves and fishes, broken human relationships, marginalized and scorned human beings, and even those who had died — and through his loving embrace offered them to the One who sent him, praying that God's loving meaning within all these creatures would be released and fulfilled. God's Spirit replenished within all whom Christ offered to the Father that fullness of life that God alone could restore. And yet his death seemed to put an end to all he had achieved.

But then the loving presence of their crucified and yet risen Lord worked within his followers an ever-deepening awareness: his death and resurrection were not the *overturning* but the *consummation* of his entire life. What Jesus did on the cross was the extension and fulfillment of his offering of our broken existence into the love of the Father all throughout his ministry. Jesus made of his suffering and death a way of handing over himself, and all he had hoped to achieve, into the hands of the One who loved him, confident in the Father's will to bring all things to fulfillment. The Father's answer to Jesus's prayerful offering was the resurrection. The resurrection showed forth the inexhaustible love that flows between Jesus and the Father, and at Pentecost Jesus poured out this Holy Spirit, this relationship of love between Jesus and the Father, to the new community of his followers. The life of the early Christian community became a visible sign within our world of a new kind of relationship — based not on power and violence but on an inexhaustible love, a level of deep understanding and communion among us whose language and medium is Christ himself.

Christ and the Holy Spirit Lead Us into God's Life

Over the decades that followed, the new community of Christ's body, the church, began to understand more, to be led by the Holy Spirit more fully into the meaning of what was happening to them through their continued fidelity to Christ. It seemed to them that just as he had done in his earthly ministry, now in his risen life, Christ was holding his people into his relationship with the Father, and that as a result the Father was re-creating them and filling them with a new identity — neither Jew nor Greek, slave nor free, male nor female, but rather all beloved children of God. Jesus's friends found themselves transformed in a way they could only explain as a new act of creation. They believed fervently that only God who created the whole universe had the power to re-create them. It seemed to them clearer than ever that their human Lord Jesus was the very meaning of God, the Word of God, expressed within the broken structures of their world — and that through Christ, God was pouring out the divine love and power and joy, the Holy Spirit, who, as the author and giver of life, could make the whole creation new.

They began, therefore, to realize that the oneness of the holy God of Israel whom they worshiped was not a mere mathematical oneness but rather a perfect and infinite unity of endlessly loving communion. They came to believe that God — who is existence itself and the cause of all that exists — is the eternal activity of self-sharing love. This is the same communion of love they encountered as they were drawn by the Holy Spirit into Jesus's relation with the Father. Jesus and the Holy Spirit seemed to Christians to be the living reflection within our world of an eternal relationship of self-giving life: the inexhaustible life of God as Trinity.

And so Christians have come to believe that God's meaning, God's Word, expressed in our world as Jesus, is the eternal coming forth of God's understanding of Godself, the Word by which God eternally knows Godself and all the ways in which creatures will come to share in the gift of existence. And likewise, the Holy Spirit, whom they now realized was the Father's delight in the beloved child Jesus and Jesus's responding love of the Father, is the eternal joy and love by which God loves Godself and all the creatures whom God knows in the Word. Herbert McCabe, a twentieth-century British Dominican, offers one of the freshest and clearest accounts of how Christians have come to think about God as Trinity.

> Let us be absurd for a minute and try to imagine what it means for God to understand himself. I don't mean try to think or understand it (of course we cannot do that). But let us try to *imagine* understanding that limitless abyss of life and liveliness, that permanent explosion of vivacity and awareness and sparkling intelligence and, of course, humor. And remember that in understanding himself God will thereby be understanding all that he has done and is doing, all that he holds in being, every blade of grass and every passing thought in your mind. The concept he has of himself in all this is his Word. This is what is made flesh and dwells amongst us in the human suffering and dying Christ. And in contemplating his life in this Word, in this concept, in contemplating all he is and all he does, God has surely a huge unfathomable joy, and immense excitement and enjoyment in all the life that is his, and all

the life he has brought into being. God takes immensely more joy in one little beetle walking across a leaf than you can take in everything good and delightful and beautiful in your whole life put together. If he gets that pleasure from one beetle he has made, think then what joy he takes in being God. This limitless joy is what we call the Holy Spirit. To be able, through faith, to share in Christ, in God's understanding of himself, to be in Christ, is to be filled ourselves also with this joy, this Holy Spirit.*

Contemplating the Trinity for Spiritual Consolation

Jesus's friends needed many years to recognize God as Trinity. Reflecting on that long transformation of consciousness can sometimes help people as they consider how they themselves may be in the process of growing into a truer and more life-giving understanding of God. Sometimes people experience God as absent or silent, yet, with gentle attention, it is often possible to help them bring to consciousness some of the hurts or deep disappointments in their life that may make it harder for them to sense God's love in their life. They may find that the silence between them and God is actually filled with a sense of anger or deep sadness that they have felt unable or without permission to speak to God.

At such times, the thought that God's own beloved child, Jesus, has been with them every step of the way, in their aloneness or in their suffering, can be a deep consolation and mo-

---

* Herbert McCabe, "Nobody Comes to the Father but by Me," chapter 9 in *God Still Matters* (London: Continuum, 2002), 105.

ment of insight. They might be encouraged in prayer to ask God the Holy Spirit to give them the sense of Christ, God's loving Word incarnate, dwelling within them and speaking on their behalf and with profound wisdom the words they would long to say but are unsure of or afraid to utter.

In this way, the mystery of the Trinity affirms for us that our lives and the life of our entire universe are embraced *within* the infinite communion who is God. In the months before she died during World War II, the French Jewish intellectual Simone Weil reflected on her growing devotion to Christ, especially in the context of her own suffering and that of her fellow Jews across Europe. It seemed to her that Christ's willingness to love in the face of hate, and on the cross to give himself in solidarity with all who suffer, is the extension within our world of the infinite act of creative love by which God embraces and sustains the universe.

> God created through love and for love. . . . He created beings capable of love from all possible distances. Because no other could do it, he himself went to the greatest possible distance, the infinite distance. This infinite distance between God and God, this supreme tearing apart, this agony beyond all others, this marvel of love, is the crucifixion. Nothing can be further from God than that which has been made accursed. This tearing apart, over which supreme love places the bond of supreme union, echoes perpetually across the universe. . . . This is the Word of God. The whole creation is nothing but its vibration.*

* Simone Weil, "The Love of God and Affliction," in *Waiting for God*, trans. Emma Craufurd (New York: Perennial, 2001), 72.

In Weil's vision, the infinite love between the Father and the Son embraces within itself, by the power of the Holy Spirit, the whole universe of creation: God, in other words, "makes room" within Godself, within the distance between God the Father and God the Son, for all beings to exist and to love. The cross is what God's infinite love looks like as it reaches into our suffering world to embrace us. Weil was filled with hope as she came to contemplate the mystery of the Trinity, certain that nothing and no one could ever be placed beyond the infinite reach of the love between God and God.

Discovering Our True Lives within God's Life

Few mystical theologians have pondered the meaning of the Trinity for our lives more deeply than Blessed Jan van Ruusbroec, a Flemish mystic who lived at the beginning of the fourteenth century. Ruusbroec longed for his readers to realize how their lives in time and space flow forth from God's knowing and loving of them within the Trinity. "For the being and life that we are in God, in our eternal image, is immediately and indivisibly united with the being and life that we possess in ourselves." Our present life in time and space, which we think of as limited within the constraints of our biology and our culture, in fact is the reflection of "the being and life that we are in God," the image or idea that exists imperishably in God's knowing and delighted loving of us.

Ruusbroec wants us to see that in every moment of our lives we can turn to God and pray for the renewal of ourselves according to God's creative idea or image of us. Our spirit, he says, "ceaselessly receives the imprint of its eternal image," and God "constantly comes to it afresh with new resplendence from his eternal birth" — that is, God's infinite understanding of God, the eternal birth of the Word, radiates at the heart of our being, renewing within us God's knowledge and love of us.

At the same time, says Ruusbroec, God's speaking within us draws us "back" into our eternal being in God's Trinitarian life, refreshing our spirit in God's blessedness. Our spirit then "flows out again with all other creatures through the eternal birth of the Son and is established in its created being by the free will of the Holy Trinity."* Ruusbroec's vision of us and all our fellow creatures ceaselessly flowing forth from God and returning to God — imaging the eternal flowing forth and return of the divine persons — helps us to sense the vibrant communion of the Trinity as the hidden or mystical rhythm within the heart of all reality.

Frank's Reflections on the Trinity and Personal Transformation

Mark's extended meditation on the Trinity invites us into the realm of experience. As he makes clear, the developed doctrine represents the early church's way of naming and describing their experience of God. For many members of the clergy, preaching about the Trinity is difficult, because the formal doctrine seems remote and detached from their experience. Even Gregory of Nazianzus, known for his passionate defense of the Trinity in five sermons, could admit that three-in-one

---

* Jan van Ruusbroec, *The Spiritual Espousals*, quoted in *Light from Light*, ed. Louis Dupré (Mahwah, NJ: Paulist, 2001), 188–89.

is "paradoxical" and not easy to take in. Many a joke has been made about the Trinity being "incomprehensible" in a popular rather than a theological sense.

Reading this chapter, I am reminded that several years ago the pastor of the church where my wife and I worship finished his Trinity Sunday sermon by inviting the congregation to look around the church and try to find some sign of the Trinity in one of the stained glass windows, or elsewhere in the building among its icons and statues and symbolic decorations. "If anyone finds a symbol of the Trinity," he added, "I will take them to lunch." During the exchange of the peace, which occurred shortly thereafter, a woman approached him and said, "We are surrounded and embraced by the Trinity, so we don't need some representation or image." The priest was convicted by the truth of her words; he announced what she had said to the congregation and later that week took her to lunch — much, I am sure, to the delight and approval of the Holy Three.

As I reflected upon Mark's words, and let them draw me into my own sense that I live and move and have my being within the life of the Trinity, I was reminded of the icon of the Trinity that is part of the visual scripture of the Eastern Church. It is a depiction of the visit of God to Abraham and Sarah, recorded in the eighteenth chapter of Genesis, in which Abraham looks up and sees three men, later identified as angels, coming to meet him. He invites them to eat, and in the icon they are seen sitting around a table under a tree. Here we have the mystery of the One and Three. In the icon, the most famous of which is that of the Russian monk Andrei Rublev, the three figures are arranged such that they form a partial circle that is completed by the person or persons standing in front of the icon. Viewers, as they ponder the scene, are drawn into the communion of the three figures, or, one might say, their shared life of love and knowing is extended to include viewers. For me, the icon speaks of invitation, of welcome and participation in the personal mystery of the Trinity that Mark so richly lays before us.

One of the freshly stated ways we are given to think about our relation to the Trinity is that the risen Christ, through his Spirit, offers us to the One he calls Father, who, in turn, through the same Spirit, restores and renews us in the fullness of life that God alone can bestow. This is indeed what Saint Paul is pointing to when he declares, "God has sent the Spirit of his Son into our hearts, crying, 'Abba! Father!'" (Gal. 4:6). Is this not Christ "in us" bearing witness with our spirit, and once again, saying yes to the Father (Abba) in the personal depths (heart) of each one of us? Is this not the baptismal relation between Jesus and the Father replicated in each one of us through the Spirt — that same Spirit who bore down upon Jesus, revealing his belovedness and evoking his answering, "Yes," his answering love. Again, when Paul cries out, "It is no longer I who live, but it is Christ who lives in me" (Gal. 2:20), the Christ who lives in me is continually yearning in love toward the Father in the Spirit, as the Father, in the same Spirit, yearns toward the Christ in us in unbounded love. The Christ in me is not some sort of set-apart presence, but an indwelling that permeates my whole being inasmuch as Christ, the Word, is the agent of creation. As such, Christ is — borrowing from Saint Augustine — more intimate to me than I am to my own self.

Creation

Creation as God's Continual Gift of Existence

Christians believe that God is the creator of all that exists. We do not hold this belief as a rival theory to any of the scientific accounts of the origin of the universe. All these scientific accounts theorize about how things in the universe began to interact, so that we arrive at the universe as we know it. Christians can happily embrace whatever seems to be the best scientific reasoning about all this. All these accounts attempt to explain in various ways how things in the universe underwent radical change. By contrast, the Christian belief in God as creator is not about any *change* in things, but about *why there are any things at all rather than nothing.*

By the mystery of creation we mean the *continuous* activity by which God holds all things in existence — not an activity that happened only at the beginning of time, but an activity that is innermost in everything causing it to exist moment by moment. The divine self-giving holds everything in being and is present at the heart of every being, as a singer holds her song in being for as long as she sings it, and is intimately present within every note of her song. Saint Thomas Aquinas says that God is present in every being, as fire is present in everything that burns. Recall for a moment our analogy in chapter 1: although an author is not *one of the things* present in the world of his novels (for he exists in a way that transcends everything within the world he creates), yet he is present at the very *heart of all things*, because he is thinking them into being and loving them into the fullness of themselves moment by moment.

One way that Christians have tried to make this clear is by suggesting that God creates the universe out of nothing — sheerly out of God's gracious love. In other words, unlike, say, the big bang or some other theory about the *transformation* of subatomic particles in the universe, Christians mean by the term "creation" not any kind of change in things that already exist, but rather the infinite divine self-giving that continuously brings reality *into* existence — rather than there being nothing at all. Everything that exists depends upon and resonates with the divine giving at its core in every moment. Saint Augustine, for instance, portrays creation as the continuous speaking of God's eternal Word at the heart of everything that exists, ceaselessly calling it by name, calling it into existence out of nothing moment by moment, calling it toward its true reality.

Because God transcends everything that exists, in the way authors transcend everything within the world of their novels, God can be intimately present *within* everything as its creative source, analogous to the way authors are present within every aspect of their novels. Thus, the Christian vision of creation leads to some wonderfully unexpected implications. We could say, for example, that everything happening in every moment is an act of God as well as an act of each creature. My writing these words at this moment is an act of God, not because God turns me into a robot and acts instead of me, but precisely because God is giving me my particular form of existence moment by moment. Thus, God is not in any form of rivalry or conflict with any creature; nor does God need to dominate or use violence to accomplish anything within the world, for God is simply thinking and loving all creatures toward their truest flourishing.

Because God is not an item within the universe, it can be hard for us to talk about God without unintentionally thinking of God as another being alongside us rather than the source of all beings. But we can say what God is *not*. For if God is the cause of everything, then God cannot, like the things that exist, be liable to fall into ruin or succumb to provocation and fall into a rage or change from being gracious to being cruel. All these are examples of changes in things that are not complete in themselves but are affected by other things. By definition God as the cause of all things cannot be affected by anything else. Otherwise, that other thing would apparently be the cause of God. Crucially for us all, the God who revealed Godself to Israel doesn't need to use power or fear or violence, because this God is the living source of everything — the God who is innermost in all things — calling them toward their fulfillment: the God who is unchangeably and inexhaustibly love itself.

Belief in the mystery of creation can be a very helpful way for people to consider the infinitely self-giving graciousness at the ground of their existence. At the heart of our lives is this ceaseless giving of God, a giving that is not in response to anything we have done or are but is simply an act of the divine love. We cannot return too often to this foundation, for in good times and in bad, the very fact of our existence can be a sacramental sign to us. Our existence marks an infinite gift; our sudden and continuous epiphany from nonexistence to existence is the sign to us of the infinite knowing and loving of God the Trinity, who delights in us.

Humanity's Contemplative Calling on Behalf of Creation

Thinking about the Trinitarian life from which all creatures flow can also reconnect us to the ancient Christian conviction that humanity has a contemplative calling, a role to play in the reverent care of creation. The existence of creation is not an inscrutable imposition of the divine will but rather a theophany, that is, the expression or reflection in time and space of the infinite act of divine knowing and loving. In knowing Godself in the eternal begetting of the Word, God also knows all the ways in which God's life can be shared in by creatures. This means that in the eternal Word dwell imperishably the divine ideas of all creatures, the divine wisdom or archetypes by which each creature will come to exist, and by which its truth is eternally sustained and known. And just as God knows the truth of all creatures in the Word, so also God eternally loves and delights in the truth of each creature in the Holy Spirit.

All creatures are held in being as God reflects aspects of God's eternal knowing and loving into the realm of time and space — just as authors reflect aspects of their own consciousness into the world of their novels. Aquinas puts it this way: "God is the cause of things by his intellect and will, just as the craftsman is cause of the things made by his craft. Now the craftsman works through the word conceived in his mind, and through the love of his will regarding some object. Hence also God the Father made the creature through his Word, which is his Son; and through his Love, which is the Holy Spirit."*

Thomas Aquinas uses the analogy of an artisan making something beautiful, just as we have used the analogy of a novelist. An artisan or novelist draws upon an idea conceived in her own mind, a mental word, as the blueprint for what she will create; and her love of this creation, her love for the way it perfectly expresses her idea, draws her idea into embodied life — her love imbues what she has made with goodness and brings it toward fulfillment. In a similar way, says Thomas, each creature reflects the Trinitarian life of God because each creature reflects within time and space some aspect of God's idea of Godself in the eternal Word, and each creature is loved toward its fulfillment by the very same love with which God loves Godself, God the Holy Spirit.

Because of this mystical trace of the Trinity within every being, we are invited to help foster the contemplative communion among all creatures, and between the creation and God. In one of the early accounts of Saint Francis of Assisi, we can see how Francis's commitment to poverty permitted his complete availability to God's beauty and goodness, which is mystically present at the ground of every creature. "Aroused by all things to the love of God, he rejoiced in all the works of the Lord's hands and from these joy-producing manifestations he rose to their life-giving principle and cause. In beautiful

---

* Thomas Aquinas, *Summa theologiae* 1.45.6, trans. Fathers of the English Dominican Province (Westminster, MD: Christian Classics, 1948), 237.

things he saw Beauty itself and through his vestiges imprinted on creation he followed his Beloved everywhere, making all things a ladder by which he could climb up and embrace Him who is utterly desirable. With a feeling of unprecedented devotion he savoured in each and every creature — as in so many streams — that Goodness which is their fountain source."*

In contemplating his fellow creatures, Francis was wonderfully attuned to the infinite divine generosity, beauty, and goodness from which all beings flow, and which radiate within every creature. In this way, Francis "followed his Beloved everywhere," recognizing in every being the loving presence of Christ the Word incarnate, in whom and through whom all creatures come to be. Inspired by Saint Francis, we might ask God the Holy Spirit to set us free from possessive attitudes toward our fellow beings, and to awaken our own hearts to the infinite divine self-giving at the heart of every creature.

We humans (and angels!), Christians believe, are called to recognize God's loving truth at the heart of every creature. How does this contemplative calling work? Think for a moment about what we know when we contemplate our fellow creatures. At the heart of every creature, God's eternal Word continually speaks the divine truth that is the very essence of each creature. When we contemplate a hummingbird or an oak leaf or friends walking together, we are not simply beholding the external form; rather, our minds receive the divine idea that God speaks at the heart of each creature, and by the light of this idea in our minds we are able, for example, to recognize

---

* Bonaventure, "The Life of St. Francis" 9.1, in *Bonaventure: The Soul's Journey into God; The Tree of Life; The Life of St. Francis*, trans. Ewert Cousins, Classics of Western Spirituality (Mahwah, NJ: Paulist, 1978), 262–63.

the brilliant iridescent whirring of wings as a hummingbird of God's own knowing and loving. Like Adam, before whom God brought each of the animals so that he might name them, we are given the wonderful privilege of hearing and recognizing God's loving communication at the heart of every being. If we are willing to ask for the grace of contemplation, we can help replenish the connection between heaven and earth — between God's *eternal* knowing and loving of every being, and every being's cherishable yet vulnerable life in time and space.

We can see a particularly lovely example of this spiritual teaching in the words of a great Anglican priest, poet, and mystical theologian, the seventeenth-century writer Thomas Traherne:

> The Idea of Heaven and Earth in the Soul of Man, is more precious with GOD than the things themselves, and more excellent in nature. . . . The World within you is an offering returned. Which is infinitely more Acceptable to GOD Almighty, since it came from him that it might return unto Him. Wherein the Mysterie is Great. For GOD hath made you able to Create Worlds in your mind, which are more Precious unto Him then those which He Created: And to Give and offer up the World unto Him, which is very Delightfull in flowing from Him, but much more in Returning to Him. Besides all which . . . a Thought of the World, or the World in a Thought is more Excellent than the World, because it is Spiritual and Nearer without unto GOD.*

* Thomas Traherne, *Centuries* 2.90, ed. H. M. Margoliouth (Oxford: Clarendon, 1958), 102 (spelling modified).

Why would Traherne believe that when we human beings reverently contemplate our fellow beings, so that our minds conceive the idea at the heart of each creature, this is "more precious with God than the things themselves"? I don't believe Traherne at all intends to denigrate the embodied reality of every being, but rather he intends to highlight the way in which our minds are able to hear the echo of God's creative idea at the core of every being. Thus, Traherne thinks, God speaks the knowable truth and beauty at the heart of all creation, and some of God's creatures have the privilege of hearing this divine idea and offering it back to God in great thanksgiving. In this way, he says, we "offer up the world unto him, which is very delightful in flowing from him, but much more in returning to him." Traherne invites us to rejoice in the flowing forth of all creatures from God into time and space, and in their return through our thanks and praise; thus we participate in drawing all beings and ourselves ever more fully within the Trinitarian communion that God longs for us all to enjoy. In a time of ecological crisis, the Christian belief in the mystery of creation holds crucial resources for our lives as spiritual weavers of creation's consummation, and as spiritual advocates of our planet's future.

Frank's Reflections on the Goodness of Creation

Mark's reflections on creation remind me of the observation of the English theologian Austin Farrer, that God created the world to create itself. Hence, the accounts at the beginning of Genesis, which unequivocally proclaim God as creator, and the understanding of evolution, which in some quarters is perceived as a threat to God as creation's source, are brought together and bear witness to the dynamic and ever-unfolding mystery of the universe and the world in which we live.

What Mark helps us to see is that creation is not simply God's action, but rather God's self-expression and the manifestation of God's goodness and love. "And God saw that it was good" (Gen. 1:25), we are told as God contemplates the world God has "spoken" into being. Humankind is then brought forth, and "God saw everything that he had made, and indeed, it was very good." The "good" that God sees is God's own goodness reflected back to God's Self, and the "very good" includes the personal mystery of each one of us. Mark describes creation as a "theophany," and it is those who have their inner eye unblinded by the Spirit who are able to see with undistorted sight, that is, in the words of the Jesuit poet Gerard Manley Hopkins, "The world is charged with the grandeur of God." We too are part of that world in which, again in Hopkins's words, "There lives the dearest freshness deep down things."*

Psalms provides a wonderful school for the training of our inner eye to perceive both the "grandeur" and the "dearest freshness" in the world about us, and in ourselves. Psalm 148, for example, calls sun, moon, shining stars, waters, earth, animals, and humankind to "praise the Lord." Note that God is not being praised because of these things but by the things themselves. By being what they are called to be, they are praising the Lord. The shining of the sun, the fruitfulness of trees, the grazing of the cattle, the flying of the birds, the young and

---

* Gerard Manley Hopkins, "God's Grandeur," Gerard Manley Hopkins Official Website, https://hopkinspoetry.com/poem /gods-grandeur/.

the old being and doing what they were created to do — each is in itself an act of praise, a lived yes to its creator. "The just man justices," declares Hopkins in a poem that begins "As kingfishers catch fire." Or, as he says earlier in the same poem,

> Each mortal thing does one thing and the same:
> Deals out that being indoors dwells.

In other words, our "indoor" or true self is the self that God knows and loves and has called into being and upholds through Christ, who "sustains all things by his powerful word" (Heb. 1:3). This self, nurtured by the Spirit "bearing witness" with our spirit, "deals out" and manifests who we are in grace and truth with a revelatory naturalness that Hopkins captures in saying, "The just man justices." The just man, in other words, praises God by acting justly and thereby inhabits who he has been loved into being. As the Spirit, the minister of communion, draws us into the force field of love, which is the inner life of the Trinity, that same Spirit works in us a communion and reconciliation of the disparate dimensions of ourselves. This work of reconciliation and inner healing is realized in spiritual freedom: "Where the Spirit of the Lord is, there is freedom" (2 Cor. 3:17), or again, "For freedom Christ has set us free" (Gal. 5:1). Francis of Assisi, whom Mark holds up to us, is an icon of spiritual freedom, "having nothing, and yet possessing everything" (2 Cor. 6:10). Because of his inner freedom and undistorted sight, Francis could see and embrace all things in a spirit of universal brotherhood.

With regard to the personal mystery of each one of us situated within the all-enveloping mystery of creation, I think of Psalm 139. Its first eighteen verses are an introspective meditation upon the intimacy of God, who searches and knows us "completely" and, as Saint Augustine would add, knows us better than we know ourselves. Again, God's knowing of us is the knowing of all-embracing and unrelenting love, which elicits awe and thanksgiving as we cry out with the psalmist, "I praise you, for I am fearfully and wonderfully made."

The Problem of Natural Suffering

Besides responding to hurtful misconceptions, Christians have also attempted to clarify the very nature of evil and suffering as part of preparing the way for our most profound belief in this area, namely, our belief in Christ. Part of the suffering we encounter in the world seems to be built into the very structure of the universe: wolves prey on caribou, tectonic plates shift and devastate homes along the fault line, viruses attack the body's health. In such cases, the ones undergoing harm are undeniably damaged, and yet the cause of the harm is simply, it seems, a part of nature being itself. The wolf that eats the caribou is being fulfilled as a wolf. The virus that sickens me is simply being a successful virus. Of course, there are certainly cases where human sin exacerbates the natural course of things — the droughts, fires, and floods that destroy whole communities are increasingly likely to be devastating precisely because of human disregard for our environment. But even apart from this human culpability, we are still faced with natural suffering, and we might well ask why God could not have created a universe that did not require such suffering built into it.

If we think about it, though, it is hard to imagine genuine wolves and viruses and tornadoes that simply remain in suspended animation, having no contact or effect on the world around them. What we would be asking for is a world without material beings at all. This observation will not be comforting to someone suffering terribly from a virus, but it does at least suggest that far from being derelict in divine duty, God intends the most complete possible fulfillment of life for the whole of the universe. God is not absent from the suffering in nature; God is present most intimately in every creature, no matter what it undergoes, always knowing and loving the truth of all that each creature could be and will be.

······· 6 ·······

Suffering and Evil

Release from Hurtful Ideas about God and Suffering

Christian faith in God's infinite goodness can often be tested by the suffering and evil we encounter. The world is deeply shadowed and devastated in ways that, Christians believe, are not natural to God's good creation. Whenever people undergo suffering or sorrow, our care for them begins attentively where they are themselves and not with the theological truths that may, ultimately, be important for their healing. Nevertheless, even in our deep solicitude and solidarity with others, we are better off knowing how the Christian tradition has approached suffering and evil: the struggles and insights of our fellow Christians over many centuries offer us powerful wisdom in times of trial.

Some of this wisdom consists in clearing away misleading preconceptions. Christian beliefs in God as creator and as Trinity crucially liberate us from any belief that human suffering is a sign of God's anger and punishment. As we saw in chapter 5 on creation, God is not one of the items of the universe, subject to creaturely passions like anger or the need for revenge. The only punitive suffering inflicted upon creatures in this world is inflicted by other creatures, never by God, for God's action within the lives of creatures is never a reaction, dependent on the creature's good or bad actions. God, Christians believe, is unchangeably Love itself. In the eternal Word, God knows each and every individual being, including all the ways in which each being struggles and sometimes becomes unable to live into its own truth; and in the Holy Spirit, God cherishes and delights in each and every individual being, loving it toward its fulfillment for all eternity.

Another preconception erroneously holds that God is simply absent, and in fact must remove Godself from creaturely experience in order for creatures to have free will. What Christians actually believe and teach is that God transcends the plane of creaturely existence, and for that reason is innermost in every creature (knowing and loving it into existence in every moment). Thus, God is *more* involved and *more* aware of every creature's suffering than any creature could be to another.

The Mystery of Human Evil

There remains, however, the far more disquieting reality of moral evil, the kind of suffering inflicted willfully through human failure to be truly human: centuries of slavery and racial oppression, trafficking of children, merchandising weaponry to foster endless cycles of violence, intentional dumping of toxic chemicals to avoid the cost of proper disposal, persistently malignant abuse and bullying that damage people for life, and on and on. The mystery of moral evil is terrible, and Christians can and must call upon God to be with us in the presence of such horrors, that we may neither seek to hide from them and avoid responsibility for helping victims nor succumb to the power of evil and allow it to persuade us of its apparent ability to defy God.

As I noted, sometimes Christians have sought to mitigate the horrific incoherence of moral evil's existence in God's world by suggesting that evil is simply the price of human free will, that God must withdraw from human consciousness in order that human beings may make their own decisions. In my view, this is an extremely unhelpful misunderstanding of the mystery of creation: God, Christians believe, is at the very heart of human consciousness and existence, continually knowing and loving the truth of each human being and calling each human being toward its truest self. God is not absent from human persons who inflict evil, because God is continuing to hold those persons in being, and indeed to love them in the truth of themselves. Their choices and actions toward evil, however, devastate the truth of themselves and make it increasingly impossible for them to hear and receive God's loving truth. Thus, their evil actions lead to their own undoing as human beings.

God's Transforming Presence in the Midst of Suffering

The most profoundly Christian response to the mysteries of suffering and evil, in all their forms, is the mystery of Jesus Christ himself, and the work of the Holy Spirit to unleash the loving power of Christ's dying and rising throughout the whole creation. In his life and in his death, Jesus refused to relinquish the fullness of his humanity, and thus with the poor he accepted the severity of nature's rigors. And in continuing to love, and to declare the truth of the One who sent him, Jesus entered into the darkness of human malignancy and evil with his loving humanity fully intact.

The fullness of humanity Jesus exhibited profoundly threatened the religious leaders and military occupying forces, who resorted to torture and execution to rid themselves of him. They enforced a status quo by the omnipresent threat of violent power, a status quo in which the deep desire to communicate and to give oneself to others (that makes us fully human) was continually defeated. Even in the face of this, Jesus boldly and passionately gave himself in love, allowing others to communicate with him and each other from a depth within themselves that they had not realized was there. He gave himself to be the language and medium of communication among his followers and between themselves and God.

All this the world's moral evil intended to silence and defeat by putting Jesus to death. God did not respond to this by rescuing Jesus from the world's enmity, nor did God respond with retributive power and vengeance — as though evil were in fact the most fundamental reality, resorted to alike by divine and human actors.

Rather, in a mystery that infinitely transcends all that the world had done or could ever do, God responded to this evil — and in this response lies God's response to all evil — by vindicating Jesus and all that he had said and done, by vindicating the fullness of his humanity, by revealing the infinite reality of the love that Christ embodied. This divine reality appears in our world as a human being defeated by suffering and evil, who

is yet alive with a greater reality and intensity of life than anyone can imagine. The mystery of suffering and evil remains,
for now, but Christians believe, and through their fidelity to
Christ experience, the reality of God's loving presence in and
with all who suffer evil, and the reality of a life and love beyond
the power of death.

The Transfiguring Power of Christ's Dying and Rising within Us

How can we understand our sharing in Christ's death and resurrection more deeply? More specifically, how can Christ's dying and rising transfigure the meaning of our own suffering —
and that of all other beings? When we think about suffering
and loss, we notice that these almost always entail a separation
from the self that we were: a relinquishment and leaving behind of what we love. But now reflect for a moment that there
is another kind of leaving self behind: for when we are in love,
we come out of ourselves and give ourselves to the one we love.
And there are times when these two ways of leaving ourselves
behind are one reality. For example, if a child runs out into
a busy street, a parent may rush into the oncoming traffic to
rescue his child. In such a moment, he risks losing his life, for
the self that he was may be left behind — and yet this giving
away of himself is a self-giving in love. His love for his child
transfigures his loss of self; in a sense, we could truly say that
suffering and evil do not take his life from him, but he gives
his life in love.

This analogy may help us to think about an even more
profound transformation of self-loss into self-giving, and an
infinitely greater power released within such an act. We know

that Jesus was thinking along these lines during the night before his betrayal and crucifixion. For speaking to his disciples, whom he now calls his friends, he said, "No one has greater love than this, to lay down one's life for one's friends" (John 15:13). Here Jesus makes explicit this holding together of the self-loss of suffering with the self-giving of love. And the love that Jesus has always lived from and for and shared with others is, Christians came to realize, the most powerful of all realities, for it is revealed in Christ to be the very life of God. Jesus identifies this self-giving love with the heart of his own agency and purpose. He does not see it as suffering only, but as the power to draw suffering into new life.

And perhaps there is a yet greater mystery revealed in Jesus's death and resurrection. For in entering freely into our world's brokenness and finitude and death, Jesus seems to have revealed a deep law written within the heart of creation — a law that had been trampled into obscurity by ages of human greed, cruelty, and violence. This deep law expresses within our world something of our creator's own life: the power of self-giving love to transfigure suffering and death into a new kind of life, the life that swallows up death, the life of our creator. But how could this be so? How could self-giving love have such power? In all suffering there is a separation from our former self, a loss, a relinquishment of all that we have been and have loved and have tried to achieve. In Jesus's dying and rising, Christians believe, God reveals to us the *deep law of our own being*, because Christ's action expresses within our world the *eternal law of God's own being* — in whose image we are created. Contemplating the dying and rising of Christ, Christians came to believe that in God the Trinity there is a likeness to what we undergo in our suffering.

In God, this is not an act of suffering but the inexhaustible act of love: God is God by giving Godself away in love. The Father gives himself away utterly so that there can be Another in God, the Beloved Child, who does not hold his equality with the Father as something to be grasped, but gives himself away in an infinitely loving expression of the Father. And over this infinite distance, this infinite relinquishing and self-giving within God, God the Holy Spirit pours out the inexhaustible love that sustains God as Trinity in Unity. All our loss and all our suffering can be embraced within the infinite self-giving of God, and in this way all self-loss among creatures can be cherishingly transformed within the inexhaustible self-giving of the Trinity. For within God all our losses are held and honored and transmuted in the life of love, for God who is love itself is not diminished but is all the more Godself in giving Godself away in love. For that is the nature of love, on earth as it is in heaven — the more love gives itself away, the more it is love itself. In God, whose very life is the infinite giving away of One to Another in love and freedom, the terrible losses and relinquishments that suffering and evil bring upon us in this world are respected and regarded with inexhaustible love, even as they are embraced within — and opened up to — the infinite divine "relinquishment" that is really infinite self-giving love, the love of God the Trinity.

Frank's Reflections on Solidarity in Suffering

Thinking of our call to be a companion in times of suffering, I am reminded of the counsel of Gregory the Great in his treatise *Pastoral Care*: "Let every Christian leader be both alongside each person under their pastoral care in compassion, and lifted above all in contemplation, so that he may both transfer to himself the weakness of others through the inner depths of his mercy, and at the same time, transcending himself, seeking the unseen through the heights of contemplation. The balance is important lest in seeking to scale the heights a leader despise the weakness of his neighbor, or in attending to the weakness of his neighbor, he lose the desire for the sublime."*

Contemplation is the ground of the Christian leader's life in Christ. The "inner depths of the leader's mercy" is born of the realization of her own weakness, and the truth of Christ's words to Paul when he prayed to be delivered from the thorn in his flesh: "My grace is sufficient for you, for my power is made perfect in weakness." As the fruit of the Spirit matures in us, we become less studied and self-preoccupied. We find ourselves more and more possessed of what I can only call "graced spontaneity." We see it in many of the saints who were able to be alongside another with an ease and naturalness that allowed the other to experience the deathless love and compassion of Christ mediated simply by their presence. Especially when we are confronted by suffering, we need to be aware that the inner depths of our Spirit-shaped mercy is what we bring, and that Christ's compassion and love can shine through simply by our being there, often in spite of the awkwardness of our not knowing what to say or do.

Saint Paul admonishes the churches in Galatia, "Bear one another's burdens, and in this way you will fulfill the law of

* Gregory the Great, *Pastoral Care*, quoted in *Celebrating the Seasons: Daily Spiritual Readings for the Christian Year*, ed. Robert Atwell (Norwich, CT: Canterbury, 1999), reading for the Saturday after the fourth Sunday before Lent.

Christ" (Gal. 6:2). The law of Christ is the law of love — the love that constitutes the relation between the diverse limbs of Christ's risen body. So it is that being alongside another in his suffering can plumb the depths of our hearts in such a way that we are intensely present with the intensity with which God is present, and both of us are one in the sufferings of Christ.

7

Jesus as the Incarnate Word

Being Drawn by Jesus into His Relationship with the Father

I wonder which stories of Jesus in the Gospels mean the most to you. At different times in my life, I believe the Holy Spirit has spoken the meaning of different gospel stories within me, helping me to meet Christ in a way that was most important to me at that time. Sometimes it has been the feeling of Jesus right next to me, teaching and helping me to pray. Sometimes I have found myself like Zacchaeus, scrambling higher among the branches of a tree, hoping somehow to catch a glimpse of Jesus as he moved through the crowds — and then astonished as he looked up directly at me and asked to spend time with me. Sometimes I have listened in wonder, the flickering torch light upon his face as he gazed into the faces of all the room, searching for some sign of what word the Father would have him speak to them — and then with a mysterious gravity and beauty the words of a parable would unfold, "There was a man who had two sons . . ." Mercy and forgiveness, welcome and healing all seem to flow from him. And above all, overwhelming abundance, inexhaustible resources, loaves and fishes and healing and life and reconciliation and peace, all somehow coming to life in those around him. Where does this overflowing generosity come from?

As we saw in chapter 4 on the Trinity, Jesus's followers found themselves drawn into his own relationship with the One he called Father. They experienced Christ as pouring out the generous abundance of this loving relationship, the Holy Spirit, within their life together as his new community, his body the church. As they entered more and more deeply into this relational life, they found that their identities as determined by their biology or cultural location were overtaken by a new identity given through their adoption as God's beloved children in Christ. This new way of existing is so liberating and life-giving that their lives seemed to them to have been newly created, an act only possible by the power of God. Because of this they came to believe that it was truly God in Godself who has come to be with us in Christ and the Holy Spirit. This meant they came to believe that their beloved friend and teacher, their human brother Jesus of Nazareth, in all his vulnerable and passionate humanity, is also the very meaning, the Word, the self-giving and self-interpreting presence of God in our world.

Who Jesus Is

Christian believers have pondered for centuries, with awe and wonder, the mystery of the incarnation, of how God has united our humanity to God's own life in Jesus. While we cannot fully comprehend the wonder of Christ as the incarnation of God's beloved Child, we *can* show that the mystery of the incarnation is *not* nonsensical. For example, some thinkers have criticized the belief that Jesus is both fully human and fully divine, saying that this makes as little sense as saying that something is both fully a square and fully a circle. There is a flaw in such a critique: squares and circles inhabit the same plane of reality, but God is not another being existing within our plane of creaturely reality. Saying that someone is both fully human and fully divine is not at all, in spite of the apparent similarity in the way our sentences work, like saying that someone is both fully human and fully alligator. Divine life is not somehow in competition with human life so that you have to have either one or the other. Divine life is the never-failing ground of all creaturely life, and therefore no creaturely existence could ever exist at all apart from the innermost presence of God within it.

This helps us see how *everything* that exists is both a creature and the manifestation of God's giving life — because God is innermost in everything, giving it its existence. But Christian belief in the incarnation says more than this about Christ, namely, that Jesus is the appearing in our world not simply of the divine giving at the heart of every creature but, even more wonderfully, the appearing in our world of God's own meaning or Word, of God's beloved Child, who expresses and communicates the entirety of God's reality among us.

Thus, the mystery of the incarnation draws us to a very particular awareness: the identity that distinguishes Jesus from John or Mary in the life of our world is the same identity that distinguishes the Word from the Father or the Holy Spirit in the eternal life of God the Trinity. In other words, that is *who* Jesus is: the eternal Word or beloved Child of God, embodying within our world, within our humanity, the same pattern of life that identifies the eternal Word in God — the perfect expression of all that God is and all that God intends. And this is why those who meet Jesus, not only in the stories of the Gospels but all through the centuries, find in him such profound understanding of themselves, such compassionate affection, such desire for their fulfillment in the deepest truth of themselves — because as the expression in our humanity of God's eternal Word, Jesus embodies God's loving wisdom for all creatures and bears within himself the life-giving meaning God intends for every being.

What I am describing here is of course the insight of centuries of Christian believers under the guidance of God the Holy Spirit, seeking ever more deeply to understand what they had come to believe had happened to them in Christ. Christians believe that Christ expresses God's infinite meaning, both within the everlasting joy of the Trinity *and* within the historical existence of our world. So, while God expresses God's meaning in every particle of the universe, when God desires to express God's meaning within the concentrated life of a single human being, what we encounter is the historical human being, Jesus of Nazareth. Jesus enacts within our human existence the same *pattern of relationship* to the One he calls Father that God's beloved Child or Word enacts eternally: this is *who* Jesus is. In an analogous way, for example, a woman might express her personhood, who she is, both within the life of her family and also within the world of her workplace — she is the same person, expressing the same identity and characteristics and passions, even though she may express her personhood by means of different activities at home and at work.

Christians have over centuries come to rule out as inadequate expressions of our faith either of two extremes: one extreme avoids the mystery of the incarnation by believing that Jesus is not really human at all but merely God appearing in human form; the other extreme avoids the fullness of the incarnation by believing that Jesus is not really divine at all but merely a good man deeply inspired by God, much like one of the prophets. Notice that both of these extremes fail to hold the most central and uniquely Christian belief, namely, that in Jesus God in Godself has freely chosen to be fully human, to share in every aspect of our existence, including all our fears and suffering, our yearnings and our hopes, our living and our dying. The other side of this central Christian belief is that in Jesus our humanity has been fully united with God. We cannot know the fullness of what this means yet, but we do know that Jesus draws us with him into his relationship with the Father. The Holy Spirit transfigures our lives, so that we recover our true identity as children who, in Christ, share in the eternal relational life of the Trinity.

Spending Time with Jesus and Learning from Him

Many people find that meditating on the stories of Jesus in the Gospels gives Christ a means of making himself more deeply known to them, and in time they often find that they are by this means enabled to sense Christ more readily in their daily lives. Christ can be asked to bring to life the particular meaning God longs for us to sense in any given passage, or the particular transformation of ourselves God longs to bring about through our prayerful dwelling within a given passage.

Because our human companion Jesus has suffered and died and is yet alive and present with us in the full force of God's life (which in our world we call resurrection), belief in the incarnation can affirm our natural desire to know Jesus in all his human struggles, and to trust that he would gladly share his experiences with us for our good and out of love for us. Sometimes we might find ourselves drawn to ask him to help us sense what was going on for him in a given moment of the gospel story. What was his passionate desire leading him toward? At other times we might find ourselves drawn to ask him to show us how he has been present with us in particular ways at different moments in our own lives. At the time, we might not have recognized these as moments of intense consciousness of Christ. But now in prayer these can become mysterious wells of meaning and new life — as Christ gradually teaches us to recognize the patterns of his presence, the unique hopes and desires he has in particular situations, and how we might be drawn to his side and share in his work.

The more Christ helps us to know him and to sense his intentions in all things, the more easily we can rejoice in his deep life-giving speaking in all things — in the beauty of creation, in the words of Scripture, in the patterns and rhythms of liturgical life, and above all in our fellow human beings. Faith in the incarnation can allow us to become increasingly aware of how all persons are profoundly Word-bearers. It is a wonderful and often startling thing to realize how profoundly Christ the Word is present in the lives of others, almost always in ways that reshape and renew our own sense of who Christ is. Sometimes this can be painful to us, especially if through upbringing or shaping experiences our perception of life has been distorted and biased. (And, truthfully, this is pretty nearly our universal human condition.) And yet, if we ask for God's grace and guidance, being confronted with the truth of Christ in another person who deeply challenges us can help us grow toward the full stature of Christ. The twentieth-century contemplative teacher Thomas Merton offers a particularly insightful and beautiful statement about this transformative encounter between Christ in others and in ourselves: "If I allow Christ to use my heart in order to love my brothers and sisters with it, I will soon find that Christ, loving in me and through me, has brought to light Christ in my brothers and sisters. And I will find that the love of Christ in my brothers and sisters, loving me in return, has brought forth the image and reality of Christ in my own soul."*

In the section below, Frank unfolds the crucial element — implicit but not explained — in this passage from Thomas Merton: the deep, transformative process by which God the Holy Spirit helps us grow into the full stature of Christ.

Frank's Reflections on Growing into the Full Stature of Christ

"We love," we are told in 1 John, "because God first loved us." Our capacity to love is woven into the fabric of our being by the Word through whom "all things came into being." What we call love is nothing less than our participation in God's life,

---

* Thomas Merton, quoted in Frank T. Griswold, *Praying Our Days: A Guide and Companion* (Harrisburg, PA: Morehouse, 2009), 153.

our being made in God's image. So it is that Paul tells us, "God has sent the Spirit of his Son into our hearts, crying, 'Abba! Father!'" The Spirit also prays within us "with sighs too deep for words" and pours God's love (our capacity to love) into our hearts. In so doing, the Spirit bears witness with our spirits that we are God's children, God's beloved.

The Spirit also plants deep within us what Saint Augustine describes as "restlessness," a yearning, a drawing beyond ourselves toward "Abba," the ground and source of all being. "Abba" is more than an intimate Aramaic form of the word "Father." It appears on the lips of Jesus as he prays from the depths of his being, "agitated and distressed" in Gethsemane. In reading Paul, we see that "Abba" becomes a Spirit-inspired form of divine address pointing to and enabling Christ to realize his Abba relationship with the Father in us. Our prayer and our practice have one goal: intimate companionship with the risen Christ such that he ceases to be an external exemplar of righteousness and becomes the deep truth of who we are, and are becoming. When Paul speaks of Christ being formed in us, and our being conformed to the image of God's Son, or again when he declares, "The life I now live is not my own, but the life Christ lives in me," he is testifying to the work of the Spirit shaping and forming us "in grace and truth," and drawing us ever more deeply into the life of the Trinity.

The consequence of the Spirit of the Son bearing witness with our spirit is freedom. "For freedom Christ has set us free," declares Paul. Freedom from what? Freedom from self-construction and self-preoccupation; freedom to become who we are as beloved in God's sight. "Where the Spirit of the Lord is, there is freedom." Such freedom, wrought in us by the Spirit, produces what Paul calls the fruit of the Spirit. What follows is not a catalogue of virtues but the description of a multidimensional character that comprises "faith, hope, love, joy, peace, patience, kindness, generosity, faithfulness, gentleness, and self-control." This is nothing less than the character of Christ — the consequence of Christ being formed over time in us.

Awakening to Christ, Who Speaks the Truth of Us

Christian mystical teachers have often pondered the various ways in which Christ's presence in our lives becomes more real to us. Frank helps us to see how these transformations could take place within us; he writes that the Holy Spirit enables "Christ to realize his Abba relationship with the Father in us." In one sense, of course, the Word is always coming forth from the Father within us, for the Word is the Father's speaking of us, calling us into our existence moment by moment. Thus, our very existence is a sign within time and space of the relationship between the Word and the Father — and that is *true of all our fellow beings*, for they are all epiphanies of the inexhaustible self-giving of the Father to the Son so that the universe may exist. But not all beings (as far as we know anyway; we may well be in for a great surprise about this!) are able to *awaken* to this relationship at the ground of their existence. This long journey of awakening is the journey of our nature as God draws us into grace; it is the work of the Holy Spirit awakening us to Christ the Word incarnate realizing "his Abba relationship with the Father in us," as Frank says. Why is this so significant?

It's so important because it allows us to be all the more available to God. And that seems very like what happens to people when they spend time with Jesus. Over time and by the grace of the Holy Spirit, we are wonderfully awakened by Christ's friendship with us, by his communication of our truth in our heart. We become aware that he is not only beside us but also within us, that he is not only present to us but is also helping us to be the fullest and most beautiful expression of his speaking presence within us. As Frank put it above, the Holy Spirit draws us into "intimate companionship with the risen Christ such that he ceases to be an external exemplar of righteousness and becomes the deep truth of who we are, and are becoming."

In this chapter we have tried to suggest how our Christian belief that Christ is the incarnation of God's eternal Word becomes a wonderfully fruitful seed of faith. For the reality and power of the incarnation are not something in the past but are present, at work within our lives and the life of the whole creation. In our companion volume, *Harvest of Hope: A Contemplative Approach to Holy Scripture*, you will find a number of meditations on the words and deeds of Jesus, all of which draw upon our faith in the incarnation of God's Word. And thus, this particular seed of faith (belief in the incarnation) can be seen growing in our reading of the Scriptures, and the harvest of hope comes as a gift of the Holy Spirit in our prayer.

8

The Death and Resurrection of Jesus

Christ's Passionate Desire

One way of contemplating the meaning of Christ's death and resurrection would be to ask Jesus to share with us the inner passion that guided him. How does he understand his calling and all that happened to him? He seems to have lived his earthly life with a deep joy in the love he shared with the One he called Father. This sense of being so unreservedly loved gives him his identity and shapes the way he spends time with others. We can imagine how remarkable it would be to have a friend and teacher like this. With Jesus, people felt able not simply to be themselves but to discover a depth within themselves they had not known was there. And this deep quality of understanding that Jesus brought out in them allowed them to be with others as they too discovered more about themselves through their friendship with Jesus. It felt as if Jesus spoke the deep meaning of their lives — as if he himself were the very word, the language, by which we could really communicate

82

with each other and by which our friendship with each other could grow. And they sensed Christ's joy in their growth.

Jesus's friends found that in his presence they could risk that fullness of humanity with one another that the world usually inhibits and distorts. Their life together enabled them to understand the mysterious wisdom in Jesus's teachings and parables, his actions and his prayers: a mysterious welling up of abundance and mercy and hope that always seems to flow through Christ and into the networks of relationship that grow around him. The loving relationship that Jesus invited people into could be seen blossoming in a miraculous abundance of food, of healing, of forgiveness, and of new life where life had been shadowed by death.

Being with Jesus makes people aware of his yearning to bring others to a wholly unexpected fulfillment of their lives — a fulfillment that seems to carry us beyond the possibilities of human achievement. Jesus knew that this consummation of our created existence could only come as a gift from God. In all his words and deeds, Jesus was holding our world up in prayer, asking the Father to bring about this fulfillment of our created existence — and to do so in ways that would open our eyes to its reality. This was his mission from the Father: to live so humanly as to release within his fellow human beings the unrealized truth of our own humanity, and the hidden abundance within all creation.

Why Did Jesus Die?

The religious and political establishment was deeply disturbed by the claim implicit in Jesus's acts, namely, that in and through friendship with himself, human beings could receive the fullness of God's blessing — apart from the established structures that the authorities wielded to control people. By publicly torturing Jesus, labeling him a blasphemer, and subjecting him to the Roman practice of state-sponsored terror and death, the authorities intended to silence Jesus and to undermine everything he had said and done.

What the authorities could never understand, however, was that — in perfect constancy with the whole manner of his life — Jesus made of his passion and death an opportunity to consummate the handing over of all that he had hoped to achieve, of all that he longed for the Father to fulfill. Christ made of his dying an offering: drawing the whole world to himself, he handed it and himself over to the Father in prayer. Jesus's suffering and death were not something God required in order to forgive and love humankind. His suffering and death were inflicted by a world that finds his uncompromised humanity dangerous and threatening. But Jesus did not simply succumb to the world's violence. By the power of true humanity that God released within him, Jesus made of his suffering and death an opportunity to put himself and all he loved into the hands of the One who loves him and sent him to us. And in this way, he opened death itself to a new meaning, a way of encountering the divine love that welcomes us and is infinitely more real than death.

The authorities' destruction of Jesus and their grotesque distortion of all that he had done would certainly, in the normal course of our world, have been successful. Jesus and his movement would have been consigned to oblivion. Given this brutal effectiveness in silencing Jesus and his followers, only something profoundly mysterious, and inexplicable in human terms, could have given rise to the rebirth of his community. Accordingly, the resurrection of Jesus points to an infinite mystery. For while Jesus's torture and death are events sickeningly familiar within the course of our world, the resurrection is *not* simply another event that happens to reverse the sequence. I do not of course mean by this that the resurrection of Jesus did not happen, but rather that its happening is of a kind we can barely begin to imagine in our present life — for it happens with the very power of God's own life.

What the Resurrection of Jesus Reveals and Accomplishes

If we refresh our pondering of the mystery of creation, we may be able to help ourselves contemplate in its full force the mystery of Christ's resurrection. It was Saint Paul who first suggested this crucial analogy. Thinking about the wonderful and mysteriously creative generosity that brought new life to Abraham and Sarah even in their advanced old age, Paul ascribes this miracle to the God "who gives life to the dead and calls into existence the things that do not exist" (Rom. 4:17). By holding resurrection and creation together, Paul helps us to avoid a calamitous misunderstanding: the resurrection, says Paul, is *not* simply another step — in this case a reversal — in our historical sequence. The resurrection of Jesus is not another event within our world such as would be the resuscitation of a corpse. Analogously, the creation of all things is not one event among others in the course of our world, but rather the giving of existence to our world. Creation is the infinite leap from nothing into finite existence. Resurrection is the infinite leap from finite existence into life with God.

The resurrection of Jesus is the appearing *within* our world of the infinitely self-sharing divine life that brings our world into existence. The resurrection is the Father's response to the prayer that Jesus had made of our world, the prayer that Jesus had made of his entire life. It is the vindication of the truth of all that Jesus had said and done and the truth of his very identity as God's beloved Child. It is a vindication achieved by projecting into the broken shards of our world the infinite life and meaning, the eternal Word, who calls all creatures into existence.

But within the world we have made, this manifestation of infinitely loving generosity takes the form of the crucified and yet living human being, Jesus. Imagine for a moment what it would be like to see the ongoing act of divine creation — to see yourself and everything around you as a continuous epiphany of divine love, a continuous presencing of creaturely existence, miraculously held into finite being out of nothing moment by moment in the loving hands of God. The resurrection of Christ is the transcendent analogy to the act of creation: instead of holding beings into *finite* existence, God in Christ holds creation into *divine* existence. We could say that Jesus appears to us, in our present world, from our own future, from the life of the world to come.

This means that his life is no longer bound within the limits of our mortal life, but has been raised into divine life, over which death has no dominion. It can be helpful to recall that finite mortal life and divine life are not simply the same kind of life, except that God has more of it than we do! The mortal life of creatures is like an echo or a reflection within time and space of the infinite and inexhaustible life of God. That is why the risen life of Jesus, which is the divine life appearing within our world, is hard for Jesus's friends to recognize or understand.

If we return for a moment to our analogy with a great novelist and the world of her novels, we can perhaps get a glimpse of what I'm suggesting. Suppose one of the characters in her novels were to die, but then in the following chapter she brings the character back to life; that would be analogous to thinking of Christ's resurrection as merely his resuscitation or return to mortal life. By contrast, suppose that one of her characters were to die within the world of her novel, but by an inconceivable act of imagination she were to *bring him from the world of her novel into the real world*, the world of her own existence as the author of all things within the world of the novel. Now her character would be truly himself and yet alive with the kind of life enjoyed by his author. Were he to appear again in the world of her novel, he would have to appear as someone who had "come back to life," that is, to life as it is known within the world of the novel. In reality, however, he would be alive with a transcendent life, the life of his author.

This is an admittedly inadequate analogy for what Christians believe has happened in the resurrection of Jesus, yet it may help us to move toward a deeper contemplation of the resurrection. Within the world we know, the world of finite creaturely existence, Jesus died. In responding to the prayer Christ had made of his entire life, the Father raised Jesus into the truth of his life in God — that is, into the truth of his full humanity that exists by participation in the relational life of the Trinity. This happens naturally for Jesus, we might say, because of who he is, because he is the eternally beloved Child of the Father in their Holy Spirit. Thus, in raising Christ from the dead, the Father brings Jesus into the everlasting truth of his own identity, of who he is. In our case, the abundant fulfillment of our humanity that Jesus had begun to awaken is poured out within us by the gift of the Holy Spirit, the joyful love of the Father and the Son, who works within us the dying and rising of Jesus, so that we may come to share by grace in his relationship with the Father.

Living into the Risen Life of Christ

Accordingly, when Jesus appears among his friends after his crucifixion, it is true that he is alive from the dead, but this both veils and unveils the actual mystery of his resurrection. It veils it because, from within our world of finite existence, it can only appear to us (erroneously) that Jesus is simply alive again with the kind of life we know; and yet the presence of the risen Christ is really an unveiling of life itself, a making present within our world, *not* of our kind of life simply resuscitated, but of the life of our Author. Our encounters with the risen Christ are transformative: they bring into our midst, within our present life, that infinite consummation of our humanity that Jesus begins to awaken within us, and that God intends us to enjoy forever in the general resurrection.

The Holy Spirit works within us Christ's dying and rising — an ongoing conversion whose beginning is marked by our baptism and whose consummation is, in the vision of God, without end. We can always turn to God and ask for a renewed sense of Christ's loving and transformative presence in our lives. It is this sense of being loved without reservation that frees us to communicate from the divine depth within ourselves. And this is what allows us to risk loving in a way that fulfills our humanity, by drawing us beyond ourselves and toward that infinite goodness who is God. This freedom to give ourselves away in love grows with the inner conviction that it is Christ who lives in us and makes within us this offering of all we are to the One who loves us — and from whom we have received everything.

In this way our ongoing participation in the paschal mystery attunes us to the deep divine rhythm of reality itself. For the whole universe is continually called into existence by the God who exists by giving Godself away in love and freedom: God the Trinity. This means that creaturely existence has at its very heart an echoing Trinitarian rhythm — of receiving all in love and giving all in love. If, as Christians believe, the life of all creatures is an echo within time and space of the Trinitarian life, then we shall discover that in giving away ourselves in love and freedom, all shall be restored in an unfathomably greater life. The death and resurrection of Jesus mysteriously speak to us of the endless self-giving of God the Trinity — and open our eyes to this self-giving as the mystical reality within all beings.

In one of her notebooks, Simone Weil likens reality to a magical gift in a fairy tale: its secret power is only released when the gift is shared and given away, and then the giver receives untold promises; but if in fear and anxiety one hoards the magical gift, then its hidden reality is lost — extinguished by the possessive grasp that can never encompass the mysterious generosity of the Giver of all gifts. Similarly, because the ever-giving love of God the Trinity flows at the heart of every creature, the divine beauty and bounty of every creature are only brought to full expression if shared and given away, received in love and given in love, echoing the very life of their divine source.

If we think about creation in this way — as grounded in the infinite generosity of the Trinity — it may help us to become more aware of our own stance toward our fellow creatures.

We may notice, for example, some inner drives toward possessiveness or anxious fear of loss — interior patterns from which Christ's dying and rising would set us free. Christian mystical theology has often suggested that the true beauty and fullness of life present within creation are shut down and silenced by human greed and misuse, but that in his life, death, and resurrection, Christ includes all creation in his self-offering to the Father; and in doing so he sets free within creation its hidden richness of meaning as cherishable gifts — meant to be given and received in love, elements of communion that echo and participate in the Trinitarian self-giving life from which they come.

Our fellow creatures bear within themselves a sacramental depth of beauty and meaning, for they and we ourselves are all elements of communion. Our freedom to attend to others, however, depends upon our own ongoing conversion. How we treat our fellow creatures and our attitudes toward them intertwine with our own identity. Thus we may find that our prayer for God the Holy Spirit to work ever more fully within us the dying and rising of Christ begins to set us free from the narrow and anxious self the world has encouraged us to be — and which diminishes our fellow creatures. We can help each other to see that as we share in Christ's death we are not simply being deprived of all things. Rather, by Christ working within us his own self-offering, our relinquishment becomes a reverent and loving handing over of ourselves and of all creation back into the inexhaustible love from which it flows, and from which it derives its true meaning. Thus, as we ourselves share more deeply in the paschal mystery, we also collaborate with Christ in liberating the creation, allowing its sacramental depths to shine with the radiance of that inexhaustible Trinitarian giving and receiving of which the whole creation sings.

Frank's Reflections on the Death and Resurrection of Jesus

Fifty-three years ago, on the very day as I write these words, I became an "ecumenical oblate" of Mount Saviour Monastery, a Benedictine community near Elmira, New York. For the previous three years I had made an annual retreat there, and it had become very much a spiritual home for me. Becoming an oblate was a formal way to acknowledge my ongoing relationship to the community and its Benedictine tradition. And so it was that I knelt before an altar in the crypt of the chapel and made an act of oblation in which I offered myself "to almighty God, to the Blessed Virgin Mary, and to our Holy Father Benedict, for Mount Saviour Monastery," and promised "before God and all the saints, the reformation of my life according to the spirit of the Rule of the same Most Holy Father Benedict."

Above the altar is a large stained glass window depicting the life of a monk and, by extension, that of oblates and other Christians who sought to pattern their lives according to Benedict's Rule for Monks. For many years I made an annual retreat, revisited the crypt, stood before the window, and reflected on the year past in relation to the life set forth in the glass panels above me.

The left-hand side of the window shows a swirl of water, below which — turned upside down — is a group of buildings representing Babylon. On the right-hand side another swirl of water, surmounted by a similar set of buildings — right side up — represents the new Jerusalem. The water signifies the mystery of baptism, and the buildings turned downward and upward signify the paschal pattern of dying and rising in union with Christ. Babylon represents bondage, and new Jerusalem represents new life and the freedom of spirit that is ours in Christ: "Where the Spirit of the Lord is, there is freedom" (2 Cor. 3:17).

As Mark has written: "The Holy Spirit works within us Christ's dying and rising — an ongoing conversion whose beginning is marked by our baptism and whose consummation is, in the vision of God, without end." It is precisely this trajectory, this life journey from birth through death into "the vision of God, without end," that the window depicts, a journey that belongs not only to monks but to us all.

Ah, yes, and the middle section of the window? This shows a spade, a ladder, and an altar from which flames ascend. The three represent body, mind, and spirit, engaged in work (*labora*), study (*lectio*), and prayer (*oratio*). Above these symbols a group of upright arrows bound together represents community, and below, a shepherd's crook stands for Christ the Good and Great Shepherd, whose loving care is reflected in the oversight of the abbot.

At turning points in my life — as a young priest, as a husband, as a father, as a newly elected bishop, as the newly elected presiding bishop and primate of the Episcopal Church — I returned to Mount Saviour and prayed before the window. And as years went by and the seasons of my life unfolded, I came to see how naive I had been in my early days, with romantic notions of who I was based upon being a monk for a week and well removed from parish responsibilities and tensions, and a household ordered to the needs and urgencies of small children. "You are not at the monastery anymore," my harassed wife exclaimed when I returned home after one retreat. Her words were very much an utterance of the Spirit of truth.

What became ever clearer with each visit to the monastery and return to the window was that dying and rising with Christ occurs daily, and is mediated by the events and circumstances of our lives. The give-and-take necessary in marriage, for example, is a succession of dyings and risings animated by mutual love. Sacrifice and costly self-giving are integral to such a relationship if it is to be life-giving not only to both partners, but to those who through blood or friendship are drawn into its orbit. Marriage and other forms of committed relationship, such as a monastic community, are for the salvation of those so committed, not just for their happiness and well-being.

Wherever we most intensely live our lives, personally and with others, the paschal mystery will reveal itself in the events, circumstances, and relationships that constitute our days and seasons. The community a pastor is called to be part of and to serve can be a fiery furnace in which the pastor's pride and vainglory are challenged by the limbs of Christ's risen body who are resistant to the pastor's self-assured giftedness. Such instances can be occasions of dying to self, or rather, our constructed selves, if they are yielded to the Spirit in the full force of their painfulness, and we resist seeking refuge in self-justifying anger or the seductive pleasure of resentment or self-pity. On the other hand, the fire can be the living flame of love revealed in a smile and a nod of encouragement from a fellow limb in the third pew in the midst of a sermon, which can release the Spirit in the preacher and provoke words of illumination that overleap the prepared text and are more a surprise to the preacher than they may be to the congregation that simply knows it has been richly and truly fed.

A passage from Scripture, or a verse from a psalm, such as "It is good for me that I was afflicted, that I might learn your statutes" (see Ps. 119:71, Book of Common Prayer), can break through an all-encompassing cloud of desolation and set us free by reorienting our attention away from ourselves and opening us to the ever-present "statute" of God's rescuing love. Then again, the inertia caused by the cross of desolation is often countered by the Spirit nudging us to rise up and do something that contradicts the negative spirit that has overtaken us; visiting the sick, baking a cake, sending an email, or digging in the garden can dissolve desolation and restore our balance. These "ordinary time" experiences, as unexceptional as they may appear, are instances of the paschal dynamic of dying and rising insinuating itself into the nooks and crannies of our lives and subtly and secretly conforming us over time to the "image of [God's] Son" (Rom. 8:29).

At this point in my life, though I am considered healthy and able-bodied, illness, injury, other signs of decline, and death itself are close at hand. With ever-greater frequency, those I count as friends and sources of wisdom — icons of stability in an ever-changing world — are passing through the narrow door of death and being born into eternity. As a result, the communion of saints becomes more and more immediate and real, and Father Damasus, who stood by me as I made my oblation those many years ago, is still calling me in his native German, "Franziskus," as I now stand before the window of his design. Work (*labora*), study (*lectio*), and prayer (*oratio*), together with the impress of many lives upon my own with their love, their painful truth, their wisdom and insight, continue to reveal Christ, the Good Shepherd, to me. Depicted as he is in a third-century statue as a Roman youth in a short tunic with a sheep slung over his shoulders, Christ refuses to remain the object of devotion but strides ahead into the future and, looking over his shoulder, gestures to me and cries out, "Follow me." And where Christ, who knows me better than I know myself, will lead me has yet to be revealed, not only in this life but also in the expansion of life beyond all that we can ask or imagine that awaits us all.

Here I am put in mind of the words of Teilhard de Chardin: "God does not offer himself to our finite beings as a thing all complete and ready to be embraced. For us he is eternal discovery and eternal growth. The more we think we understand him, the more he reveals himself as otherwise. The more we think we hold him, the further he withdraws, drawing us into the depths of himself."*

---

* Pierre Teilhard de Chardin, *The Divine Milieu* (New York: Harper, 2001), 114.

Salvation

The Wonder of What God Does for Us Surpasses Understanding

As the people of God journey through time, we are always learning more about how God is perfecting all beings. We only learn about this because Jesus sends the Holy Spirit into our common life as Christians, and the Spirit draws us into Christ's relationship with the Father. Our belief in salvation, namely, that "In Christ God was reconciling the world to himself" (2 Cor. 5:19), is a prime example of faith in search of understanding — for we have hardly begun to comprehend the fullness of what God is doing for us in Christ.

Unlike our belief in the Trinity and in the incarnation, our faith in salvation has never received a particular formulation at a general council of the church. In fact, over the centuries, Christians have used a great variety of images to express our faith that the incarnation, life, death, and resurrection of Jesus are "for us and our salvation," as we say in the Nicene Creed.

Even the terms we use suggest different understandings of what Christ has done for us. For example, the word "salvation" derives from the Latin word for health and well-being. The word "redemption" implies the payment of a ransom in order to release those held captive. "Reconciliation," by contrast, suggests some form of mediation and peacemaking between those who are at enmity. And the term "divinization" implies that in Christ we are made partakers in the very life of God. So, salvation, like all mysteries of faith, is too marvelous to be fully conceivable in any single concept.

For that very reason, it can be helpful to draw upon other Christian beliefs to help us think more adequately about salvation. Some of the more exuberant imagery used by our forebears can be misleading or even hurtful if it is taken literally or as the exclusively true account of salvation. So, how can other elements of Christian belief help us clarify our thinking about salvation?

Let's take, for example, our belief in the Trinity, namely, our belief that Christ draws us into the infinite communion of the divine life. This life is, we believe, relational, a communion of love and freedom among the divine persons. On earth, Jesus builds up his body, the church, by weaving our network of human relationships into the divine relations of the Father, Son, and Holy Spirit. Our common life, by the power of the Holy Spirit, becomes a sacrament of the life of God the Trinity. How might this belief help us think about salvation? It certainly points us toward the notion that salvation means sharing in the life of God, and also that our *way* of sharing in God's life is communal or relational. In other words, we share individually in salvation because we are drawn into the communal life of Jesus's body: the church.

Second, because of our belief in the incarnation, namely, the assumption of our humanity into union with the Word, we also believe that God, in Christ, has drawn the whole creation into union with divine life. This suggests that we might want to avoid thinking of salvation as pertaining exclusively to human beings, but rather as including in some manner the whole creation.

Third, because of our belief that the God whom we meet in Christ is the very One who creates heaven and earth (and is not therefore one of the things that exists but the reason why they exist), we also believe that God is not subject to any needs nor to changing passions as creatures are, but is simply and unwaveringly self-giving love. Among creatures, when someone wrongs another, we may demand recompense and punishment because our life, being finite, has been diminished in some way, and we may also be overwhelmed by hurt or anger. But neither of these things could ever be true of God, whose existence is infinite, inexhaustible love and who is subject to no power or passion but the inner rhythm of God's own being, which is divine love itself. For this reason, it seems fitting that we *not* think of salvation as satisfying a divine need to punish and impose suffering and death in order to be willing to forgive and love humanity. In fact, it is not God who crucifies Jesus but we humans.

Sin's Story of Salvation

This is a particularly important observation because much of the language and imagery that Christians have inherited pictures the suffering of Jesus as imposed upon him as a punishment for human sins, or as a sacrifice that God demands in order to reestablish justice in the universe, or to compensate God for human wrongdoing. This imagery was ubiquitous in the ancient Near Eastern world, so it came ready to hand when early Christians began the long journey toward a deeper understanding of what God was doing in Christ. And yet the language of an implacable divine wrath implicit in such ways of thinking about Jesus's suffering and death should arouse our suspicions. If we recall chapter 3 on revelation, we can sense the toxic seepage of our fallen natural *misunderstanding* of God as it disfigures these approaches to Christ's passion. For what we have here is really *the story that sin likes to tell about itself and about God* — a story that avidly magnifies the importance of sin, whose terrible significance forces God to become angry and demand an awful punishment. Sin's distorted vision leads to an ugly irony: a theory of salvation that viciously perpetuates a fearful enmity between humanity and God, the very enmity that salvation was meant to overcome.

Julian of Norwich, the late medieval mystical theologian, was acutely insightful about how sin prevents us from believing in God's love and lures us into a false understanding of salvation. Sin operates like a nightmare whose terror can grip us even after we awake. Sin does indeed have whatever real power we creatures allow it to have in manipulating us toward unreality. But sin has no reality or power in comparison with God's eternal and infinite love. For sin is a parasite living off the fear and anger of God's human creatures while God's wisdom and love radiate at the heart of our creaturely existence, always drawing us toward what is truly real: the goodness, truth, and beauty of God — to share in which God creates all beings.

All this should help us realize that salvation is not God's plan B, not a workaround God had to come up with after being surprised by an outbreak of sin in our world. That would certainly be sin's own story, but it is not love's story. Sin leads us to focus our attention on how bad we are, and it warps its account of salvation around ourselves and our iniquity. The previous chapter on the death and resurrection of Jesus should orient us toward a very different vision of salvation. In this view, Christ's suffering and death is in no way something that God needs or demands; Christ's mission from the One who loves him and sent him to us is simply to be fully and vibrantly human, and so to make possible our own growth into the truth of ourselves as God has always known and loved us.

Love's Story of Salvation

In love's telling, salvation is really the story of God's eternal desire to give existence to what is not God, in order to bring all creatures to share in the perfect love of the divine life. The mission of Christ is to mend and perfect the openness of creation to this inexhaustible divine giving, which has never ceased to pour love into our lives, even when we have failed to accept that love. Living and loving as a true human being does lead Jesus to persecution and execution. Yet this is not something the Father demands but rather the result of the world we have made — where being fully human threatens the power structures that dominate our world.

The Letter to the Hebrews offers a helpfully nuanced way of thinking about the powers that dominate our world. "Since, therefore, the children share flesh and blood, [Jesus] himself likewise shared the same things, so that through death he might destroy the one who has the power of death, that is the devil, and free those who all their lives were held in slavery by the fear of death" (Heb. 2:14–15). The passage clearly understands the devil to be the enemy of our humanity, who uses our fear of death to dominate and distort our choices and actions. Notice, however, that in this account evil or the devil certainly has no power to thwart God, nor any right to dominate us, but rather *uses our fear of death* to manipulate and enslave us. But how does the death of Jesus lead to the destruction of this dominating fear?

Saint Paul tells us that what we call "death" directly results from sin, from the way sin infects our experience of reality. Perhaps we can think about this by asking how life in paradise, before the Fall, might have reached its fulfillment — before what we call "death" shrouded our existence. In other words, what might it have been like to hand ourselves over in love, to God and to each other — without that act of handing over being shadowed by the fear of death?

The story of the garden of Eden conveys Israel's conviction that humankind is created for relationship with God, and that apart from this relationship we lose the continual God-ward momentum that sustains our true humanity. We could think of it like this: the truth of who we are exists most authentically in and through the friendship God extends to us; but if sin undermines our trust and love for God, then our life and all we are become subject to the mortal biological substructures of our earthly life. So, the end of our natural earthly life, which might have been a means for us lovingly to entrust all that we are into the hands of God, now becomes what we call "death," with all its fearful loss and separation. Thus, sin has made it almost impossible for us to believe that our mortality could be an act of loving self-surrender that would have allowed us to emulate the very life of God the Trinity.

But what if someone could undo death from within? What if someone's loving relationship with God were able to reach beyond the ending of our biological life, so that our mortality were no longer the ending of the relationship with God that gives us our very personhood, our true life?

The passage quoted above from the Letter to the Hebrews suggests that Jesus's mission is precisely to share our humanity in its present condition, subject to death. But because Jesus lives from and for the love of the One who sent him, he is able to make of our death exactly the kind of self-giving offering in love and freedom that consummates our humanity. In doing so, Jesus destroys death as we presently know it. Jesus makes it possible, through our baptismal identification with his dying and rising, for our own moment of transition to become not our extinction but our consummation through communion with the One who knows and loves us perfectly and forever. And so it is that Jesus's entire ministry and his death become the means by which Jesus heals our human condition from within.

In the resurrection of Jesus, the Father's infinitely loving *acceptance* of Jesus's self-offering breaks into our world. And this acceptance by the Father fulfills Christ's humanity by bringing him to live directly from the very life of God. In this way, the life, death, and resurrection of Jesus releases humankind from its subjection to the dominating fears that imprison us and our world in sin, and *also* draws our humanity into the self-giving relations of God the Trinity: life that is unbounded by death.

Once more, in Christ, our true personhood can flourish and grow into maturity through our friendship with God, our participation in the divine communion.

To be saved, I suggest, means to be drawn into ever-deeper communion with God. In this way human relations, and relations between humanity and all our fellow creatures, become more and more assimilated to and gloriously permeated by the infinite relations of God's Trinitarian life. Salvation reaches its consummation in the life of the world to come, in the new creation, when God will simply be the life we lead.

Frank's Reflections on Christ's Self-Giving, and Our Dying and Rising in Christ

As I reflect upon what Mark sets before us in chapters 8 and 9, "The Death and Resurrection of Jesus" and "Salvation," respectively, the following words of a prayer come to mind: "Lord Jesus Christ, you stretched out your arms of love on the hard wood of the cross that everyone might come within the reach of your saving embrace."* As Mark points out, there are different ways of interpreting Jesus's death in relation to us, but the overarching reality that confutes any notion of propitiation or satisfaction to placate an angry God is love. Saint Catherine of Siena famously declared that love, not nails, held Jesus to the wood of the cross. This reminds me of the Byzantine painted cross of San Damiano, before which Saint Francis was praying when he heard the voice of Christ telling him, "Go, repair

* Book of Common Prayer, p. 101.

my Church." Jesus's arms, though clearly nailed to the cross, are welcoming and embracing, rather than suffering. And the blood that surrounds the nails is a sacramental sign of the self-gift of the One who said, "No one has greater love than this, to lay down one's life for one's friends" (John 15:13). Perhaps Francis, in the uncertainty he felt about the direction of his life, felt drawn into those welcoming arms of love, which then prepared him to receive Christ's call.

It has been said that Jesus's inner struggle, "distressed and agitated," in the garden of Gethsemane, was the heart of his passion. There he sought desperately in prayer to find his bearings in relation to the will — the loving desire — of the one he addressed as "Abba." This Aramaic word for "Father" is used by Jesus only in the Gospel of Mark: and it is here, as Jesus finds himself "grieved unto death." "Abba," coming from the lips of the Master, became a form of address sacred to Saint Paul and the early church. It signified the intimacy and mutual love that passed between the Father and the Son in the Holy Spirit. Those who through baptism were now limbs of Christ's risen body and indwelt by "the Spirit of the Son" and drawn into the life and deathless love of the Trinity were empowered to address God as "Abba." "When we cry, 'Abba! Father!' it is that very Spirit bearing witness with our spirit that we are children of God" (Rom. 8:15–16).

Throughout Jesus's ministry, which followed his baptism, he is described as going apart to pray. Such times of withdrawal allowed him to reground himself in who he was and to hear echoes of the voice he heard as he emerged from the Jordan, "You are my Son, the Beloved; with you I am well pleased." Most intensely in the garden, he once again sought that confirming voice as he faced the darkness that lay ahead. The devil, whom, Luke tells us, after Jesus's struggle in the wilderness, "departed from him until an opportune time," must have been close at hand in the garden whispering expediencies such as, "If you follow this path and desert your disciples, they won't be able to carry on. They are not ready. Just gather them up while it's still dark and head back to the safety of Galilee." "Abba," Jesus prays, "for you all things are possible; remove this cup from me; yet, not what I want, but what you want" (Mark 14:36). His humanity recoils, yet love carries him forward, and perhaps it is the ministering angel who appears in Luke who whispers, "You are Beloved," and gives him the courage to rise and go forward into what lies ahead, inextricable as it may be.

Jesus, however, is not a tragic victim. In the full force of his freedom, and animated by the love he shares with the Father, he cries out, "I lay down my life in order to take it up again. No one takes it from me, but I lay it down of my own accord. I have power to lay it down, and I have power to take it up again. I have received this command from my Father" (John 10:17–18).

In an early English poem, "The Dream of the Rood," the cross is given voice and describes Jesus's approach to his death "with great zeal."

> Men carried me there on their shoulders, until
> they set me on a hill,
> Enemies enough fastened me there.
> I saw the Saviour of mankind hasten with
> great zeal,
> As if he wanted to climb up on me. . . .

He stripped himself then, a young hero — that
    was God almighty —
Strong and resolute; he ascended on the high
    gallows,
Brave in the sight of many, when he wanted to
    ransom mankind.
I trembled when the warrior embraced me.*

    The words of Jesus, the Good Shepherd, from the Gospel of John, and the cross's description of Jesus, the young hero/warrior leaping onto the cross — these underscore his full agency in the face of his passion. The ransom he brings through his self-gift of his humanity back to the Father is, in Mark's words, "to live so humanly as to release within his fellow human beings the unrealized truth of our own humanity, and the hidden abundance within all creation." This description reminded me of Jesus's declaration in the Gospel of John, "I came that they may have life, and have it abundantly" (John 10:10). All of life, its ups and downs, its joys and sorrows, its triumphs and failures, is the stuff out of which our humanity is shaped and matured. Whether or not we acknowledge as a spiritual journey this process of unfolding and living into the personal mystery of ourselves, it is a path we are all obliged follow — either with bitterness and resentment that things are as they are, or in a spirit of patient endurance, such that Saint Paul commends in his letters. "Suffering produces endurance," he tells us, "and

---

    * Anonymous, "The Dream of the Rood," in *Old and Middle English, c. 890–1450: An Anthology*, ed. Elaine Treharne (Oxford: Wiley-Blackwell, 2010), 118.

endurance produces character, and character produces hope, and hope does not disappoint us, because God's love has been poured into our hearts through the Holy Spirit that has been given to us" (Rom. 5:3–5).

Note that endurance produces its own fruit. Though experienced passively, it can work its own mystery within us and thereby produce character — that is, a depth and fullness of being rooted in God's love poured into our hearts, which enables us in turn to love. Hope is what happens to us when we are disabused of our own sufficiency through suffering and find ourselves open to the Spirit, who moves within us "with sighs too deep for words." By endurance, Jesus tells us, "you will gain your souls" (Luke 21:19).

The cross involves endurance; it is the "narrow door" through which Jesus, and all of us, must pass in order to enter the open pasture of resurrection. The narrow door, however, confronts us not only when we approach our hour of death but also in the multiple dyings and risings we pass through in the course of our daily lives. "Unless a grain of wheat falls into the earth and dies," Jesus tells his disciples, "it remains just a single grain; but if it dies, it bears much fruit" (John 12:24). This is the dynamic of the paschal mystery that we celebrate in the sacrament of baptism, not simply as a ritual or a pious metaphor, but as the path each one of us is obliged to follow. "When you were buried with [Christ] in baptism, you were also raised with him through faith in the power of God, who raised him from the dead" (Col. 2:12). What follows is the living out of that pattern as the grain of my life is plunged into the darkness of the soil of loss and uncertainty, where it remains as I endure as it is broken open and new life slowly emerges, producing the fruit of new vision, wisdom, self-knowledge, compassion, reverence for others and the world in which we live.

One of the things that often has to die, as it did for Saint Paul, is a sense of our own virtue by which we judge ourselves as superior to others. Sadly, religion is frequently deployed to give us the illusion that we are the Pharisee and not the tax collector in Jesus's parable (Luke 18:9–14). But here I am reminded of the insight of Julian of Norwich that sin is necessary in that it causes pain that acts as a purge, allowing us to know ourselves as we truly are. And, like the tax collector in the parable, to ask for mercy. Perhaps the pharisee in us can then recognize the tax collector with compassion, and as a brother in his poverty of spirit, rather than as the object of our contempt. Sometimes we have to go backward in order to go forward, and even our sins can become the teacher we need to "come to ourselves," like the prodigal son in the parable, and then to go home to "Abba," who has been waiting for our return with yearning love ever since we "wandered far in a land that was waste."* Such is the paschal pattern woven into our lives. The seed of our self-sufficiency dies, or rather is broken open and produces "much" fruit — that is, the fruit of the Spirit of the risen One renewing our minds and extending his arms of love to us and through us to others.

The paschal mystery, though differently described, is a universal pattern found in all the great religions and can be summed up in the paradox that one must lose in order to find. The experience, however, can be painful and disorienting, and yet there is manna in the wilderness to sustain us along the way.

* Book of Common Prayer, Reconciliation of a Penitent, 450.

The very capacity to endure is a gift, as is the inchoate sense of hope buried within it. "In the depth of winter, I finally learned that within me there lay an invincible summer." These words of the existentialist writer Albert Camus speak to us all.

If we are not consumed by a sense of our righteousness, we can, by default, be mired in preoccupation with our sinfulness, such that an awareness of God's mercy and Christ's welcoming arms of love only increases our fixation on our unworth. We see something of that struggle wonderfully captured in George Herbert's poem "Love (III)," which appears in chapter 2. Mark warns us against focusing our attention on how bad we are, and losing sight of the overleaping, self-giving life of the Trinity, experienced as love poured into our hearts by the Spirit.

"Why are your sins more important to you than they are to me?" These are the words a friend of mine heard in his mind as he was taking a shower during a retreat. At that moment, he told me, his only thought was to get the stinging soap out of his eyes and certainly not matters spiritual. Why there and then and not when he was recollected or at prayer? God is a god of infinite surprise, and often humor. Just when we are least "spiritual" or in a godly frame of mind, the Lion of the Tribe of Judah, as Christ is named in Revelation, bounds into our consciousness. My friend's response was to laugh, and in that moment to experience liberation. "For freedom Christ has set us free" (Gal. 5:1), or again, "Where the Spirit of the Lord is, there is freedom" (2 Cor. 3:17). What can be more liberating from self-judgment and the inverse pride of one's sinfulness than the deathless, reckless, boundary-crossing, insistent love of God, whose ways confute all our notions of blame and punishment, and whose thoughts are not our thoughts, and whose love, like his peace, passes all understanding? Here I am put in mind of the words of one of Mark's friends in the Spirit, Herbert McCabe, OP: "When God forgives our sin, he is not changing *his* mind about us; he is changing *our* mind about him. He does not change; his mind is never anything but loving; he *is* love."*

* Herbert McCabe, *God, Christ, and Us* (London: Continuum, 2005), 16.

Grace and Human Flourishing

Is There More to Life Than We Can Imagine?

Grace is our name for God's constant presence to us and within us. In mysterious and often startling ways, the life of God transforms us and moves us toward a divine future we cannot now imagine. Grace, we could say, is the beginning in us already and now of our life in God. And this is of course a mystery we can barely conceive and rarely dare to hope for with all our hearts.

The possibility of God's presence at work within us right now touches a deep longing and half-hidden expectation. Part of what we half-guess and hope for is that there is more to us, more to our future, than we presently understand. And that someone or something will awaken within us that bright beauty and goodness we hope is really there — though the circumstances of life may have made it impossible for this hidden reality to shine. Over centuries of friendship with Christ, Christians have come to believe that this shining goodness that

God brings to life within us is both truly our own and also God's gift to us. In the section below, we want to ponder some of the mysterious wonder that makes God's grace beautifully elusive to our ordinary understanding — though there is nothing we would rather understand more than this.

Why Grace Is Hard for Us to Think About

We might begin by listing some of the features of grace we would like to ponder more deeply. For instance, could there really be aspects of us that only come to life in the presence of God? How could these enhancements of our lives be both truly our own and truly divine? Can grace lead to our mending and the forgiveness of our sins? What is grace "for" and where will it lead us?

The very definition of the word tells us that the action of grace within the world is entirely God's free gift and is in no way dependent upon some prior action or merit of our own. We can never emphasize too often that *God simply gives us this transforming love* because God is everlastingly love itself and in love with all God's creatures. Perhaps that's what makes grace elusive to our usual modes of thought — the sheer gratuity and infinite generosity of grace stretch far beyond our comprehension.

When we think about God helping us to discover and become ourselves, we can sometimes be misled by our common experience of how we help each other. I remember with affectionate exhaustion, for example, teaching my children to ride a bike. Running alongside them while holding them steady and upright, I had to judge the exact moment to let go so that they could take over and begin to ride the bike themselves. And this is true in many ways. For children to grow up, parents often have to step aside and let them discover their own agency.

So does God, like a loving parent or a good friend, need to step aside in order for us to grow up? Not at all! God is not another being alongside us who somehow needs to withdraw for us to act freely of ourselves. God's action in causing us each to exist moment by moment is precisely what allows us to be ourselves and to exercise our free agency as rational creatures. God is always present in our actions and, indeed, the cause of our actions for the simple reason that God is causing us to exist, giving us the gift of ourselves in every moment.

This means that when we speak of God's grace at work in our lives, we don't mean that God is more present during times of grace and less present at other times. God is unfailingly in love with all that exists and never ceases to be innermost in all things. Rather, by grace we mean that God is awakening *us* to the divine giving at the heart of our lives. By grace we become more attuned and more actively responsive to what God is giving us to be and to become. To understand more clearly and to embrace more fully God's dream and hope for each of us is a life-enhancing and life-transforming gift.

God draws upon the infinite knowing and loving of Godself, of all the infinite wonders and aspects of the divine life, in order to create each being with its own unique way of reflecting the beauty and goodness of God. The Christian belief in creation is not that God knows and loves each creature because it exists, but rather that each creature exists because God knows and loves it — as the unique, unfolding expression in time and space of God's knowing and loving of Godself. *Grace happens as we awaken to the particular epiphany of God that we each represent.* That is why to be

fully alive by grace is to become increasingly aware of that divine
calling toward the infinitely understood and cherished reality of
oneself that exists imperishably in the heart of God.

Frank's Reflections on Grace as Forgiveness

"Can grace lead to our mending and the forgiveness of our
sins?" Pondering Mark's question, from earlier in this chapter,
I am drawn to a text from the Apocrypha that has made its
way as a canticle into Lenten liturgies in both the East and the
West: "Immeasurable and unsearchable is your mercy, for you
are the Lord Most High, of great compassion, long suffering,
and very merciful, and you relent at human suffering. . . . And
now I bend the knee of my heart, imploring you for your kindness. I have sinned O Lord, I have sinned, and I acknowledge
my transgressions. . . . I earnestly implore you, forgive me,
O Lord, forgive me. For you, O Lord, are the God of those
who repent, and in me you will manifest your goodness" (The
Prayer of Manasseh).

What is uppermost in this text is the "immeasurable and
unsearchable" mercy of God. And it is with awareness of that
mercy that the penitent is able to recognize her sins, confident
that God will manifest God's goodness in forgiveness. This
awareness and confidence are the fruit of grace working deep
within us: first through illumination, as the Spirit of truth reveals our distance from who we, in God's imagination and love,
are and are called to be. Having been made in God's image and
growing in likeness, we are "conformed to the image of [God's]
Son" (Rom. 8:29). We are like the prodigal in the parable, who
"traveled to a distant country" and there squandered his inher-

itance "in dissolute living." Through the Spirit interceding for us "with sighs too deep for words," we "come to ourselves" and wake up to the disorder, the addictive pattern of thought or behavior that imprisons us. We see the self-obsession that distorts our vision and makes us fearful and suspicious of others and the world in which we live and move and have our being. This awakening, or "sting of remorse," to use the language of Ignatius Loyola, can come in many forms: from another person in the form of a word, a silence, a look; from a book, a poem, a passage of Scripture; from, as it did for the prodigal, a sudden inbreaking of awareness — an interior voice that says, "What are you doing? Stop! Wake up," or, as for a man I know who had descended into the depths of dissoluteness and despair, a voice that said simply, "You are loved." All this is the outworking of grace: the ever-active goodness and love of the Trinity in which our every moment is embraced, sustained, and upheld. What is so important here is that because we are so deeply loved and indwelt by the Spirit, it is God's act of love to reveal to us the ways in which we have strayed from our true selves. It is never God's intention that by acknowledging our sins we become immured in self-directed hostility, but rather to see that our glimpse of sin is being given to us by the One whose mercy is "immeasurable and unsearchable." To be given the grace to "bend the knee of [our] hearts" and to see our sins in their true light is, at the same time, to open the way for God's mercy and forgiveness to set us free and to restore us to our life in the Trinity and, therefore, to our true selves. All this is one continuous action, one unified outpouring of the divine *agapē*.

Julian of Norwich tells us that "sin has no kind of substance, no share in being, nor can it be recognized except by the pain which it causes. And it seems to me that this pain is something for a time, for it purges us and makes us know ourselves and ask for mercy."* In other words, the pain of coming to ourselves in our sinfulness is a stage, but not the stopping point, in the unfolding mystery of forgiveness and reconciliation. Elsewhere in her *Showings*, Julian tells us we need to fall, "for if we did not fall, we should not know how feeble and how wretched we are in ourselves, nor, too, should we know so completely the wonderful love of our Creator."†

"Where sin increased, grace abounded all the more" (Rom. 5:20). Once again, it is through grace that we are able to "come to ourselves" in the vulnerability of knowing ourselves as sinners, and in so knowing encounter the fierce embrace of the waiting Father's deathless love.

Grace is mysterious because it doesn't play by our rules or adhere to our assumptions about how God should act in our lives; grace, as Mark says, is "beautifully elusive." "The wind blows where it chooses," Jesus tells Nicodemus, "and you hear the sound of it, but you do not know where it comes from or where it goes. So it is with everyone who is born of the Spirit" (John 3:8). Grace moves freely, often imperceptibly, sometimes as a subtle breeze and at other times as a raging gale. Grace is the action upon us and within us of the One who says,

> My thoughts are not your thoughts,
> nor are your ways my ways. (Isa. 55:8)

Something of the free-ranging nature and unpredictability of grace is captured in the startling words of the French poet

---

* Julian of Norwich, *Showings* (New York: Paulist, 1978), 148.
† Julian of Norwich, *Showings*, 300.

and philosopher Charles Péguy: "Grace is insidious. When it doesn't come straight it comes bent, and when it doesn't come bent it comes broken. When it doesn't come from above it comes from below."* So it is that grace can ever surprise us and catch us off guard by the strange routes it chooses to invade our minds and hearts in order to break us open to the divine generosity and goodness that surpass anything we can ask or imagine. And, as this happens, we know deep within us that our sins are met with compassion, not with blame.

I quoted earlier the wisdom of the Dominican Herbert Mc-Cabe, that when God forgives our sins, "he is not changing *his* mind about us; he is changing *our* minds about him. He does not change; his mind is never anything but loving. He *is* love." This love is the life of the Trinity, the living water "gushing up to eternal life" offered to us by Jesus and poured into our hearts by the Spirit, and flowing forth from our hearts as "rivers of living water," vibrant and alive with the immeasurable and unsearchable mercy grace has worked into the fabric of our lives.

Grace as the Beginning of Our Life in the Trinity

So, finally, we must ask: what is this power of grace that seems to make us all the more ourselves, even as it draws us beyond ourselves and into our common life in God? Grace is our name for what happens to us when we accept the transformative power of God's infinitely self-giving life, the life of the Trinity. For we are always astonished anew when we consider that

---

* Quoted in Martin L. Smith, *Compass and Stars* (New York: Church Publishing, 2007), 89.

the life God shares with us so freely is a life that lives by giving itself away, by inexhaustible generosity: the Trinity exists precisely by the infinite power of the divine persons to give themselves away to each other in love and freedom. It is this same power that brings things into existence out of nothing, and in resurrection raises creatures from the death of their mortal life into the boundless life of God. Unlike the acts of creation or resurrection, the fullness of grace does not overtake us all at once. But it is the same infinite power of God's giving life, transforming us and moving us, through the healing of our life together, toward the truth of ourselves in God.

In Christian mystical theology, our forebears have spoken of grace as the deepening recognition that we are always in Christ and he in us, and that God the Holy Spirit is continually pouring out within us the loving relationship between Jesus and the Father. Grace, we could say, is God loving us into and through a transition, God transforming our natural human condition so that we become sharers in God's condition — which is a life of inexhaustibly loving communion. We might think of grace as fitting us for a journey into the world of the Trinity. We do not leave our humanity behind. Rather, our way of being is extended into a realm of infinite generosity in which the truth of our humanity is finally achieved.

Christians came to speak of God drawing our humanity toward its unknown consummation in terms of the "interior missions" of the Word and the Holy Spirit. Think of how a good friend who has profound expertise and wisdom in some field is able to share her perception with you. And because of this friendship, your usual way of understanding things is liberated from whatever biases or limiting prior experiences might hinder your mind. In a much deeper way, God the Word eternal graces our minds with a share in God's own knowing of all things. And in an exactly parallel way, God the Holy Spirit impassions our hearts, liberating them from small meandering desires that reach toward the world around us in possessive and limiting ways, and draws our love toward the ultimate Goodness, who is present in all things as their desirability. We are set free from turning our world into idols, and our capacity extended to know and love and to act in accordance with God's deeper wisdom and more passionate desire.

The great mystical teacher Saint John of the Cross ponders these interior missions of the Word and Holy Spirit, seeing in them not only the liberation and extension of our knowing and loving, but something yet more wonderfully mysterious. John thinks that when God draws our knowing and loving to share in God's own knowing and loving, God is in fact *helping us to participate in God's eternal giving of Godself to God*. God the Trinity *exists* by means of this inexhaustible self-giving communion of knowing and loving; and, says John, God graces our humanity with a share in this divine self-giving, precisely so that we can enter into the infinite joy and fulfillment of giving God to God.* Contemplating God's desire to share the wonderful beauty of God's life with us can be profoundly consoling and strengthening — especially perhaps in times of difficulty when little in our ordinary lives seems to communicate to us much sense of the extraordinary or the hopeful.

In fact, a deeply useful aspect of our daily prayer may be asking God to show us and guide us toward the elements of our life that we may be invited to offer to God — perhaps by means of loving others more profoundly, working more steadily for

---

* See Saint John of the Cross, *Living Flame of Love* 3.78.

their just treatment, or struggling alongside them in solidarity. In many ways, God the Holy Spirit may open our eyes to behold the grace present to us in the manifold life of the world around us, inviting us to receive this grace — and to work alongside Christ, making of all things gifts that share in the inexhaustibly abundant giving and receiving, which is the very life of God. In this sense, the mystical truth of life comes home to us: all is grace.

The Church and the Sacramental Life

FRANK T. GRISWOLD

A Wonderful and Sacred Mystery

In this chapter I want to reflect upon the church as the body of the risen Christ whose limbs and members are themselves sacraments, that is, "outward and visible signs" of Christ's reconciling and deathless love.

A prayer from the Gelasian Sacramentary, a collection of liturgical texts from the early church, begins, "O God of unchangeable power and eternal light, look favorably on your whole church, that wonderful and sacred mystery . . ." In the seventh or early eighth century, when this sacramentary was composed, the "whole church" embraced the churches of the East and the West. The Great Schism of 1054 between Rome and Constantinople had yet to occur, and Martin Luther and the Reformation were even further into the future. The prayer has made its way into contemporary liturgies. It is the collect appointed for ordinations of bishops, priests, and deacons, and the conclusion to the prayers of intercession, "for people everywhere according to their needs," which are part of the Good Friday Liturgy in the Book of Common Prayer. And so it is that at ordinations and on the day we call to mind the outstretched arms of Jesus upon the cross embracing the world and its people, we celebrate the life of the church, "that wonderful and sacred mystery."

Throughout my ordained ministry I have reflected upon "that wonderful and sacred mystery" as it was expressed for me as rector of a congregation, as bishop of a diocese, and as presiding bishop and primate of the Episcopal Church. Over the years my sense of the church has expanded and been challenged by the reality that the gospel is not an abstraction. It is embodied in the lives of women and men who are being shaped by differences of race, culture, life experience, worldview, and historical circumstances, and who often have vastly different understandings of what constitutes the church and authentic expressions of Christianity.

In a second-century text entitled *The Shepherd of Hermas*, the author encounters a beautiful woman who identifies herself as a figure of the church. She tells Hermas he has treated her as a whore because he sought to use her for his own ends. Her words struck deep within me as I realized that my vision of the church was very much determined by my own predilections: a particular liturgical style, the language of the Book of Common Prayer, a theology rooted in the fathers of early church, a critical view of Scripture, a high sacramentalism, a preference for "What is the risen Christ up to?" rather than "What would Jesus do?" My temperament also had its part to play. I preferred open-ended exploration rather than things being neatly defined and pinned down. In short, I had my own personal image of what the church was and needed to be to satisfy my spirit and way of coming at the world. I too was guilty of using the church for my own ends. I had created an idol, a golden calf, so to speak, which shielded me from the sacred mystery of the church as it existed in God's imagination, which stretches well beyond the secure limits of my own imaginings.

As seasons of ministry unfolded — each with its own demands and invitations — to an enlargement of my vision of the church, I found myself turning, again and again, to Saint Paul and his understanding of the church as the body of Christ. I also asked myself: How did he arrive at such a dynamic vision? Might following his path illumine my own?

First, I noted Paul's description of his life prior to his conversion. "You have heard, no doubt, of my earlier life in Judaism. I was violently persecuting the church of God and was trying to destroy it. I advanced in Judaism beyond many among my people of the same age, for I was far more zealous for the traditions of my ancestors" (Gal. 1:13–14).

What strikes me in this passage is the intensity of both Paul's violence against the church and his piety, which was more zealous than that of most of his contemporaries. Did the thorn in his flesh, which he prayed to have removed, as he tells us in Second Corinthians, already exist as a source of shame, and was his intense religious practice a way to offset a sense of his imperfection?

In the Acts of the Apostles we find Paul assisting at the stoning of the deacon Stephen, who is described as having "the face of an angel." As Stephen defends himself before the high priest and the council, we are told that those who heard him "could not withstand the wisdom and Spirit with which he spoke." As well, we are told that Paul approved of his being stoned, but it is hard to imagine that Paul was not deeply affected by the radiance of Stephen's face, the convicting power of his speech, and his compassion as he prayed to the Lord to forgive those who were stoning him. Without realizing it, Paul had been exposed, in the person of Stephen, not only to a devout follower of Jesus but to Christ himself. What he sensed in Stephen was therefore a threat to Paul's carefully constructed fidelity to the "tradition of my ancestors." Those who belonged to the Way — an early name for Christianity — were, therefore, dangerous and needed to be dealt with as enemies.

Following Stephen's death, a severe persecution began, and Paul was "ravaging" the church and dragging men and women off to prison. Was his ferocity against followers of Jesus an effort to stamp out the threat they posed, particularly in Stephen, and to bolster the sense of identity he derived from his rigorous religious practice?

On the road to Damascus, the threat is brought to the surface and exposed by the one he fears most (Acts 9:1–19). "Still breathing threats and murder against the disciples of the Lord," Paul is overcome by light flashing around him from heaven. Falling to the ground, he hears a voice addressing him in his Jewish name: "Saul, Saul, why do you persecute me?" Paul asks, "Who are you?" The reply comes, "I am Jesus, whom you are persecuting." Suddenly the implanted word of the *Logos*, the Word who indwells creation, the Spirit of the Son who prays within us "with sighs too deep for words," breaks loose within him and converges with the experience of Stephen as a living witness and icon of Jesus. As this happens, Paul's former life collapses: his piety is shattered and the carefully constructed self that offset the shame of his thorn falls to the ground along with him. Paul undergoes a psychic death; his old life is over.

Reflecting upon what was surely his own experience, Paul later writes: "If anyone is in Christ, there is a new creation: everything old has passed away; see, everything has become new!" (2 Cor. 5:17).

The encounter on the road is Paul's second meeting with Jesus, the first having been his meeting with Jesus present in the person of Stephen. "Why are you persecuting *me*?" Jesus asks, not, "Why are you persecuting *my disciples*?" Jesus here proclaims his presence in his disciples. We might ask if this is the origin of Paul's understanding of the church as Christ's body, of which we, through baptism, are limbs, bearing in the fullness of our humanity and singularity the "real presence" of the risen One.

Christ then instructs Paul; he says, "Get up and enter the city, and you will be told what you are to do." Unable to see, he is led into Damascus, where "for three days he was without sight, and neither ate nor drank." Those three days — an echo of Jesus's three days? — must have seemed an eternity. What would happen next? Would he see again? Would he who led the way with letters from the high priest now be led by others for the rest of his life? Why had Jesus not told him what he was to do there and then when he spoke from the heavens?

The scene then shifts to a disciple, Ananias, who is instructed by the same voice from heaven to go and lay hands on Paul and restore his sight. Ananias objects, given what he knows about Paul and his mission from the chief priests. Christ makes it clear that the persecutor is to be his chosen instrument. Ananias obeys and, no doubt with fear and trembling, lays hands upon the head of Paul, saying, "Brother Saul, the Lord Jesus, who appeared to you on your way here, has sent me so that you may regain your sight and be filled with the

Holy Spirit." And immediately, "something like scales fell from [Paul's] eyes, and his sight was restored. Then he got up and was baptized, and after taking some food, he regained his strength." And so it was that Paul passed from an interior death to newness of life.

What strikes me as I read this account is that Paul's liberation is not a repeat of the voice from heaven. Rather, it is mediated by a disciple who addresses him as "brother" and lays very human, and quite possibly trembling, hands upon his head in a Jewish gesture of blessing. Once again, it is Jesus, present in a disciple — a limb of his risen body — who acts through the reluctant obedience of a follower. It is in the voice of Ananias that the Word speaks.

Paul's understanding of the church as the body of Christ was for him more than a metaphor: it was the consequence of what he experienced in Stephen, in the voice on the road to Damascus, and in the words and actions of Ananias. The church by its nature is sacramental, as Christ is present within those who are its limbs and members. And it is in the interaction of its members, led by the Spirit of the Son, that the church manifests God's unrelenting desire for the full flourishing of the whole creation and all of humanity.

The energy that constitutes the church and sustains it in witness and mission is love. What we know of and experience as love is God's self-gift. Being formed by love, and enabled thereby to love, is what it means to be made in God's image. "We love because [God] first loved us." Love is the name we give to our participation in God's own life. "God is love, and those who abide in love abide in God, and God abides in them" (1 John 4:16). To love is not some sort of discretionary virtue or a task that Christians "ought" to do. Love is integral to our being fully human and alive. It is not primarily an emotion, but rather the foundation upon which the substructure of our personhood is secured. "Everyone who loves is born of God and knows God" (1 John 4:7). Put another way, everyone who loves is being who they are created to be. Their spirit is bearing witness with the Holy Spirit, who pours the love of God — that is, our capacity to love — into our hearts. Here I am put in mind of the late Dom John Main's definition of prayer: "Prayer is an openness to love on every level of our being." Though all of this may sound idealistic, nonetheless love is the heart and center of the church's life — that wonderful and sacred mystery. As well, love is the heart and center of *all* human life.

Love Is in the Gifts of the Spirit

Love is refracted in the form of many gifts. "There are varieties of gifts, but the same Spirit: and varieties of services, but the same Lord; and there are varieties of activities, but it is the same God who activates all of them in everyone. To each is given the manifestation of the Spirit for the common good" (1 Cor. 12:4–7). Note that the gifts are variously distributed by the Spirit. They are not for the personal aggrandizement of those who receive them, but rather are given for the common good.

The various gifts are allotted to each person individually and woven into the fabric of the lives of the limbs of the body. Different gifts are embodied in different people. Here tensions and judgments can occur, as certain gifts, and those who receive them, are perceived as more valuable than others. And as we know from Scripture and the history of the early church, dissension and conflict within the body have been present from the beginning, with the most obvious clash being between those who came from Judaism and those whose background was gentile.

Paul faced this challenge head-on. Within the body of Christ, as in the human body, difference is essential, as is the ability of the members to work together for the good of the whole. "And if the ear would say, 'Because I am not an eye, I do not belong to the body,' that would not make it any less a part of the body. If the whole body were an eye, where would the hearing be?" (1 Cor. 12:16–17). Paul develops his vision of the ecclesial body further, observing that no body part can say to another, "I have no need of you." All parts, "the honorable and less respectable . . . the greater and inferior," are "indispensable" to the body's health and integrity. He goes on to say, "But God has so arranged the body, giving greater honor to the inferior member, that there may be no dissension within the body, but the members may have the same care for one another. If one member suffers, all suffer together with it; if one member is honored, all rejoice together with it" (1 Cor. 12:24–26).

Rowan Williams once observed that in baptism, we are bound together in solidarities not of our own choosing. In other words, baptism into Christ initiates a person into a community of difference drawn together by the Spirit, who is the minister of communion and mutual love. The body of Christ is more a laboratory than a refuge, in which the Christ in me meets the Christ in you and is present in the other, often in ways that can catch us by surprise, and question or shatter some stereotype or bias we have long held. I have no doubt that sophisticated Jerusalem was put off by Jesus's being from Nazareth — "Can anything good come out of Nazareth?" — his dress, and his Galilean accent. Incarnation does not always make things easy.

Here I am put in mind of Father Zossima in Dostoyevsky's *The Brothers Karamazov.* "Love in action is a harsh and dreadful thing, compared with love in dreams." Life as a limb of Christ's risen body is costly and demanding. But then, baptism *is* about dying and rising with Christ. It *is* about the transformation of hearts of stone into hearts of flesh that are able to embrace the Christ in others in all their provocative singularity. The fathers and mothers of the desert spoke of one's monastic cell as a furnace in which the purifying fire of the Spirit accomplishes its work of interior transformation. The same can be said of that expression of Christ's body in which I am called to live and move and have my being; it is a laboratory and a furnace.

As a parish priest, I had to contend with those who, though faithful, found my ways of liturgy not to be their ways. I well recall one man who at the exchange of the peace dropped to his knees and held an open hymnal over his head to protect himself from assault by another limb of the body. He referred to this moment in the liturgy as "The Kiss of Death"! Though I offered fervent prayers that he might leave the congregation and find a happier church home, he stayed put and became even more stalwart in his opinions. Then one Sunday as he was leaving church, my prayer was answered, not by his announcing that he was leaving the parish, but by a sudden change of heart — my heart — when I heard a voice within saying, "He is for your salvation, saving you from self-satisfaction and vain glory." Suddenly I saw him in a different light: as an old man for whom, in a world of change, an unchanging liturgy was a source of stability and strength. Much to my surprise, I found myself looking at him with compassion and understanding, rather than anger. Grace often catches us off guard to let us know that illumination is gift rather than achievement. I now wonder if, while I prayed he might leave the parish, the grace of Christ working in him made him more resolute in staying, which was for his salvation and mine as well. I have no doubt my ability to see him with compassion was worked in me by the very same grace.

This lesson of the indispensability of every member of the body, even as the "eye" may look askance at the "hand," applies also to factions and parties within the church. It applies as well to the historic divisions within the body of Christ whereby a whole community of eyes says to a community of hands, "We have no need of you. Our theology and practice are superior and more valid than yours." I am very mindful of the idolatry of one's religious tradition, and how easy it is to become imprisoned by it. Then, from an assumed superior position, we become condescending and judgmental and cry out with the Pharisee in the Gospel of Luke, "God, I thank you that I am not like other people." Here "other people" can stand for another church or denomination, or a particular group within our congregation or ecclesial household.

It is also the case that there are expressions of Christ's body in other parts of the world where culture and tradition have led to a different application of the gospel in response to the realities of everyday life. From our "enlightened" perspective, these brothers and sisters in Christ who see things differently than we do are considered backward or naive. And yet, they too are for our salvation and are indispensable if the body is to be whole, and thereby serve as a sacrament of Christ's presence in the lives of very different and distinct women and men around the globe and in the house next door.

In the midst of our evaluations and judgments of our sister and brother limbs, the Spirit unites the body and orders its limbs such that the "fullness" of Christ is revealed in the mystery of communion. This communion transcends our natural affinities; it is in communion that we, the diverse limbs of the body, "come . . . to maturity, to the measure of the full stature of Christ," as we are told in the Letter to the Ephesians. "But speaking the truth in love, we must grow up in every way into him who is the head, into Christ, from whom the whole body, joined and knit together by every ligament with which it is equipped, as each part is working properly, promotes the body's growth in building itself up in love" (Eph. 4:11–16).

Coming to maturity and growing up in all ways into who we are called to be in Christ is a *corporate*, rather than an *individual*, process enacted by God through the Word in the power of the Holy Spirit. From the perspective of Scripture, there is no such thing as a freestanding individual. To be sure, though our relationship with God is intimate and personal, our growth in maturity involves our relationship with others through whom we are shaped and formed and conformed to the One who is more intimate to us than we are to our own selves. Such again is the sacramental nature of the church and its members, who together reveal the presence of the One who proclaims, "Abide in me as I abide in you" (John 15:4).

All this being said, I am reminded that in virtue of the *Logos*, the Word, being the agent of creation, all creation and all humanity have received life through Christ. "All things came into being through him, and without him not one thing came into being. What has come into being in him was life, and the life was the light of all people. . . . From his fullness we have all received, grace upon grace" (John 1:3–4, 16). Christ is not only the agent of creation who "sustains all things by his powerful word" (Heb. 1:3), Christ indwells the universe as Wisdom who "pervades and penetrates all things" (Wisd. of Sol. 7:24).

The Jesuit poet Gerard Manley Hopkins wrote a commentary on the *Spiritual Exercises* of Saint Ignatius Loyola. In it he declares that "God's utterance of himself in himself is God the Word, outside himself is this world. The world then is word, expression, news of God. Therefore, its end, its purpose, its purport, its meaning is God, and its life or work is to name and praise him."* Hopkins points to the reality that the world is sacramental and revelatory, and that the Word addresses us through creation.

> The heavens are telling the glory of God;
> and the firmament proclaims his handiwork.
>
> (Ps. 19:1)

Another Jesuit, Pierre Teilhard de Chardin, puts it this way, "The cosmos is fundamentally and primarily living. . . . Christ, through his incarnation is interior to the world, rooted in the world in the tiniest atom."†

The early fathers listened to the universe. Cyril of Jerusalem, for example, meditates upon the various aspects and uses of water, concluding, "In the face of all these marvels, who can fail to adore their Creator?" Or again, reflecting upon the "tiny

---

* Gerard Manley Hopkins, "Notes on the Spiritual Exercises: The Principle or Foundation," in *Gerard Manley Hopkins: A Critical Edition of the Major Works*, ed. Catherine Phillips (Oxford: Oxford University Press, 1986), 282.

† Pierre Teilhard de Chardin, *Human Energy*, trans. J. M. Cohen (New York: Harcourt Brace Jovanovich, 1969), 23. And also, *Science and Christ*, trans. René Hague (New York: Harper & Row, 1968), 36.

lyre in the breast of a cicada,"* Gregory of Nazianzus asks, "Who has arranged things in such a way that this little creature gets excited in hot weather and fills the woods with its music and accompanies passers-by with it? . . . It gives me joy to speak of these things because they unfold the greatness of God."

"Contemplation is the highest expression of man's intellectual and spiritual life. It is life itself fully awake, fully active, fully aware that it is alive. It is spiritual wonder. It is spontaneous awe at the sacredness of life."† These words of Thomas Merton in *New Seeds of Contemplation* remind us that in contemplation our life in Christ deepens. "Spiritual wonder" overtakes "the dullness of our blinded sight," and we see the world and one another in the light of the Word, who sustains and indwells the cosmos. As Clement of Alexandria names it, the Word "tunes" the cosmos, including the "little cosmos" of our humanity.

Because baptism formally constitutes the church as Christ's risen body and acknowledges the indwelling Word as the way, the truth, and the life, the lives of its members are no longer those of freestanding individuals. Rather, they are diverse and interactive particles suffused with "the boundless riches of Christ" (Eph. 3:8), sustained in a force field of deathless and all-embracing love. Baptism is an acknowledgment of the presence of Christ ever within us, albeit hidden and unacknowledged.

---

* This and the following quotation are found in Thomas Spidlik, *Drinking from the Hidden Fountain: A Patristic Breviary* (Kalamazoo, MI: Cistercian Publications, 1994), 258.

† Thomas Merton, *New Seeds of Contemplation* (New York: New Directions, 1961), 1.

In the third century, Origen of Alexandria described this reality thusly. "Each of our souls contains a well of living water. Within it is buried the image of God. . . . For the Word of God is present there, within us, and his work is to remove the earth from the soul of each of us, to let the springs of water gush free."* Origen identifies Christ, the Word, as "our Isaac," drawing on Genesis 26:18, in which Isaac unblocks wells that had been stopped up by the Philistines. This process of unblocking can be painful and costly because much of what blocks the living water within us is the refuse we have accumulated over time. This waste is so much a part of us that it can be difficult to acknowledge and relinquish. Here I think again of Paul and his dying and rising. His self-constructed righteousness is cast aside as the living water bubbles up from within and we hear his cry of liberation, "For freedom Christ has set us free" (Gal. 5:1).

"Seeds of the Word," to draw from Justin Martyr, have been planted within all of us by the Word through whom all things have their being. Baptism builds upon this truth. All creation, by its very existence, is in Christ, who is the Word. Therefore, in some sense all of humanity is within Christ's risen body. Baptism involves coming to consciousness and ordering our lives in union with the Word planted within us and "growing up in all ways into Christ." This is a lifelong process of becoming under the aegis of the Spirit, who pours the love of God, that is, our capacity to love, into our hearts. The church, in baptism, makes explicit what is implicit in all humanity. As T. S. Eliot put it, there are signs — "hints and guesses" — of the Word in other traditions with their different scriptures and symbol systems.

* Origen, quoted in *Celebrating the Seasons*, ed. Robert Atwell (Harrisburg, PA: Morehouse, 2001), 388.

When we celebrate the Eucharist, we are participating in the sacramental expression of the ongoing work of the Spirit. Here we encounter the risen Christ in Scripture and in the limbs of Christ's body gathered together to celebrate and yield themselves to the driving motions of the Spirit and to share the sacred meal, with the bread and wine being signs of our mutual indwelling: he in us and we in him.

This sense of mutual encounter and indwelling mediated by the sacraments was present in the early church. "All that was present in the Redeemer has passed over into the sacraments," declared Leo the Great.* And Saint Ambrose, in his commentary on the Gospel of John, declares: "You have shown yourself to me, O Christ, face to face. I have met you in your sacraments."† Here the sacraments are seen as extensions of the gospel and acts not only of the church but also of the risen Lord, who is the true minister of all sacramental rites. "It is no longer I who live, but it is Christ who lives in me," Paul declares in Galatians 2:20. Christ, in bread and wine, imparts his life to us, just as the food we eat imparts life to us. Saint Irenaeus bears witness to the intimate union with Christ effected through the Eucharist in this reflection.

> When we drink the cup at the eucharist, in which the wine has become Christ's blood, his blood mixes with our blood, and they become one. Equally, when we eat the bread which has become the body of Christ, his body mixes with our body, and they become one. This is how,

---

* Quoted in Geoffrey Wainwright, *Doxology: A Systematic Theology* (New York: Oxford University Press, 1984), 71.

† Quoted in Frank T. Griswold, *Praying Our Days: A Guide and Companion* (Harrisburg, PA: Morehouse, 2009), 55.

week by week, we are redeemed from sin. . . . And in this
process we become part of Christ's body and blood, unified with one another in him. . . . Thus in sharing Christ's
body and blood, made from bread and wine which are
fruits of the earth, we are brought into harmony with
the whole of God's creation. In that simple act of receiving the eucharist we participate in reconciling God with
God's world.*

Some years ago, a Latin American evangelist who had been
educated in Anglican schools told me that when in his evan-
gelistic crusades he uses highly charged language about Jesus
as our personal savior, it is those formed by the Eucharist who
intuitively understand what he is saying. As one so formed,
I well understood this phenomenon of what happens to me,
and those around me, "week by week."

"Week by week" underscores the formative effect of the
Eucharist because grace is developmental over time. Through
this repeated pattern of worship week by week, we grow more
fully into who we are called to be, not so much as we would like
to be but as the divine imagination, through grace, is calling us
to become. You might say, we are being fed in order to grow
into the fullness of our unique "limbness" within Christ's risen
body. This is not, however, a solo accomplishment. Union with
Christ is also union with "one another in him." We are united
with Christ present in the other limbs in all their diversity, and
reminded that it is together that we grow to maturity through
the love that binds the body together.

* Irenaeus, quoted in Griswold, *Praying Our Days*, 71.

Though profoundly corporate, the eucharistic encounter is as well deeply personal. As Father Richard Meux Benson, founder of the Society of Saint John the Evangelist, tells us, "Each communion should be, as it were, adding some fresh paint to the image of Christ within our souls. As each touch of the artist adds some fresh feature to the painting, so each communion is a touch of Christ, which should develop some fresh feature of his own perfect likeness within us."[*]

Jesus's use of bread and wine, that is, "the fruits of the earth," draws creation and human agency into the realm of the sacramental and disclosive. We find this in the gospel: word, touch, water saliva, mud, bread and wine, as well as simply being present, are all deployed in the service of manifesting God's reign. They "speak." They serve as a form of language beyond words in that they convey "presence." In consequence of the resurrection, Christ can use anything to manifest his presence.

At the same time, being limbs of Christ's risen body and developing a "likeness" to Christ carries with it an assignment. Saint Augustine often expressed the view that we are all the body of Christ, and that in us the work of the incarnation goes forward; for in Christ we are taken, consecrated, broken, and given to others as a means of grace, and a gift of God's love.

Over the years, I have been shocked, amused, and in awe of the wild and startling ways Christ has chosen to show up to illumine, convict, or companion me, and by the singularly inappropriate — from my point of view — vehicles Christ has

[*] Richard Meux Benson, "Of Communion," in *The Religious Vocation* (1939; reprint, Eugene, OR: Wipf & Stock, 2020), 160–61.

chosen to get my attention and break me open to an enlargement of his truth. The Lion of the Tribe of Judah was not above
using bubble gum — a huge and ever-growing pink bubble of
which exuded from the mouth of an altar server in the midst of
a solemn liturgy — to shake this bishop loose from his liturgical
rectitude. On that occasion, the "real presence" of Christ, giving me just what I needed, was mediated by pink bubble gum
even more than by the elements of bread and wine.

The formal sacraments of the church, be they counted as
two or seven, are enactments of different dimensions of the
gospel, and all find their way back to the Word incarnate, who
is, in the fullness of his divinity and humanity, the sacrament
from which all sacramental life in its many forms flows. But
why stop at a fixed number when we are surrounded by what
we might think of as everyday sacraments? That Jesus chose
a meal as the medium of his continuing presence points us to
the potential sacramental reality of all meals, if only we are
graced by the Spirit to perceive it. Indeed, life shows us how
everything can be caught up into Christ's continuing work of
proclamation, healing, and reconciliation.

The Spirit of Prayer

Frank's Reflections on Prayer

Thomas Merton was once asked by a conference attendee for some advice on how to pray. Merton answered with one word, "*Pray!*" I think his advice meant we are simply to turn to God in a stance of openness to the motions of the Spirit, who prays within us "with sighs too deep for words" (Rom. 8:26). Gabriel Marcel, a French writer and philosopher of the last century, spoke of *disponibilité*, that is, an interior state of *availability*. Though our individual prayer practices vary from person to person and from time to time, at the heart of them all is the call to *disponibilité*, as our spirits are available and open to the Holy Spirit, who, like the wind, "blows where it chooses." Saint Francis of Assisi encouraged his followers to believe that what we must desire above all things is to have the Spirit of the Lord, and his holy manner of working. As we learn to be available to the Spirit, our prayer becomes increasingly an interior disposition, and part of our ongoing everyday life. Any deep and intimate human relationship calls for attention and nurture. This call for attention and nurture is also at the heart of our relationship with the Divine. "Prayer," Julian of Norwich reminds us, "unites the soul to God." And as this union unfolds, a naturalness and spontaneity, that is, a graced unselfconsciousness, develops as our communion with God in Christ is deepened and matured in the Spirit.

As we reflect upon our journey into the mystery of prayer, we might begin by looking at some of the roadblocks or detours that can appear along the way. One is that we live in a culture that highly values setting goals and achieving them. Therefore, it is quite natural for us to approach prayer as a challenge and another skill to master. Perhaps the most essential and liberating thing we can learn about prayer comes from one who called himself "the least of the apostles," Saint Paul, who tells us that "we," and he includes himself, do not know how to pray "as we ought." His sense, then, is that our prayer comes as we turn to God out of our poverty, rather than out of a desire for mastery and achievement.

"Pray simply," advised Saint Macarius of Optino, a nineteenth-century Russian Staretz. "Do not expect to find in your heart any remarkable gift of prayer. Then you will have peace."* And yet, it is precisely the ego-driven desire to possess this "remarkable gift" that can undermine our being available, in simplicity and with open heart and hands, to the mystery of prayer as it unfolds within us.

---

* Quoted in *The Time of the Spirit: Reading through the Christian Year*, ed. George Every, Richard Harries, and Kallistos Ware (Crestwood, NY: St. Vladimir's Seminary Press, 1984), 12.

Before we move beyond self-consciousness about our particular way of praying, we might notice a tendency we have to watch ourselves at prayer and to assess our "success" or "failure." We may be thinking, perhaps somewhat unconsciously, that if we devote a portion of our busy day to prayer, we ought to receive some reward: an insight, an illumination, a mystical experience perhaps, to validate our efforts. I take comfort in the confession of Saint Catherine of Siena, who said that when she observed herself at prayer, she spoiled it. She named the self-preoccupation that can so easily turn our attention from God, and God's desire, to ourselves.

We can be helped here if we ask ourselves a question posed by Saint Augustine: Am I looking for consolation, or for the God of consolation? Am I, however imperfectly, oriented in patient trust toward God's desire and whatever God may choose to reveal or bestow? *The Cloud of Unknowing*, an anonymous guide to contemplative prayer dating from the late fourteenth century, advises us to go about our spiritual work with "courtesy" and not snapping like a "greedy greyhound" at the hand of grace, eager for our own satisfaction.

Saint Paul tells us that Satan can masquerade as an angel of light (2 Cor. 11:14). The name Satan means "accuser" or "adversary," who, according to the author of Revelation, is "the accuser of our comrades . . . / who accuses them day and night before our God" (Rev. 12:10). Alas, many, when they turn to prayer, do so not in the presence of God but rather in the presence of the inner accuser, who tells them that their efforts are superficial, immature, unworthy of God's greatness, or, most damning of all, imperfect. This inner accusing voice telling us we *ought* to have been more centered, *ought* to have been less distracted, *ought* to have been less self-focused, *ought* to have had more fervor, can cripple us and imprison us in a cell of frustration and hostility directed against ourselves that blocks and holds at bay the ever-present compassion and goodness of God.

Another way to describe Satan the accuser, this harping inner voice of judgment, is as "the enemy of our human nature." This comes from Saint Ignatius Loyola and his *Spiritual Exercises*. The "enemy," whom Jesus calls "the father of lies," deals with us by way of distortion and untruth; that judgment overrules compassion in the heart of God is the "enemy's" fundamental lie. Ignatius understood all too well that this force can deceive and entice us and draw us away from our true selves, as we are known and loved by God.

Having looked at some of the impediments that we can encounter along the pathway of prayer, we return to Saint Paul and his insight about prayer, and particularly about the relation between our prayer and the Holy Spirit. In Romans Paul tells us that "the Spirit helps us in our weakness; for we do not know how to pray as we ought, but that very Spirit intercedes with sighs too deep for words. And God, who searches the heart, knows what is the mind of the Spirit, because the Spirit intercedes for the saints according to the will of God" (Rom. 8:26–27).

These words most likely reflect Paul's own experience. In Galatians Paul describes himself, prior to his conversion, as having "advanced in Judaism beyond many among my people of the same age, for I was far more zealous for the traditions of my ancestors" (Gal. 1:14). Given this admission, Paul's liberation from his driven and self-constructed piety and his ability to proclaim that he doesn't know how to pray "as he ought" are all the more powerful and liberating for us. What Paul discovered, and invites us to make our own, is that prayer is not primarily something we do ourselves. Rather, it is the work of the Spirit praying within us, "with sighs too deep for words."

The seventeenth-century priest-poet George Herbert sums up Paul's teaching on prayer in a single line in his poem entitled "Prayer (1)." Prayer, he tells us, is "God's breath in man returning to its birth." Prayer is God's action, God's breath within us, before it is a decision we make or an act we perform. Prayer is always at work within us, below the level of our consciousness with "sighs too deep for words." In virtue of our creation through the Word, the "Spirit of the Son" occupies a privileged place in our hearts and prays within us. Here the heart is understood, as the ancients understood it, as the individuating core and center of our personhood, rather than simply as the seat of our emotions, which is our more common understanding.

The psalmist cries,

> "Come," my heart says, "seek his face!"
> Your face, LORD, do I seek. (Ps. 27:8)

And so it is that God draws us beyond ourselves through the agency of the Spirit, who whispers over and over, "Seek my face, seek my face, seek my face," until our spirit yields and "bears witness" with the Spirit, responding: "Your face, Lord, do I seek." This self-transcending yearning toward God, or one might say, toward "the source of all being," is part of how we have been created, our DNA, if you will. It is also the work of the indwelling Christ, who, through the Spirit, enlivens and orients our spirits toward God as we are joined with his, and together we cry, "Abba, Father."

The capacity for prayer is an aspect of the life we share in the Trinity with the Father and the Son in the Holy Spirit. It is the consequence of being indwelt by the Word, "by whom all things were made." This being so, prayer belongs to humanity as a whole, rather than being a practice restricted to particular religious traditions.

Origen of Alexandria helped many to understand that anyone who prays shares in the prayer of the Word of God, who is present even among those who do not know him, and is never absent from anyone's prayer.* This third-century theologian who, though maligned and declared by some a heretic, continues to have a significant voice in the ongoing conversation around theology and the life of the Spirit. In his treatise *On Prayer*, referenced above, Origen declares that prayer, as a capability, belongs to the whole of humanity. More than that, he understands prayer, along with Saint Paul, as our participation in the prayer of Christ, the Word of God, who prays within us. The capability to pray, which is an aspect of being made in God's image through the agency of the Word, belongs "even to those who do not know" God. The impulse, the urge to pray takes many forms; speech is only one of them. At the heart of this urge, this impulse, dwells the Word of God, the Eternal Son.

---

* Origen of Alexandria, *Origen: An Exhortation to Martyrdom, Prayer, and Selected Works*, trans. Rowan Greer (Mahwah, NJ: Paulist, 1979), 100.

Julian of Norwich, the anchorite born in the middle of the fourteenth century, wrote of her mystical encounter with God in her *Revelations of Divine Love*. In *Showings*, God declared to Julian: "I am the ground of your beseeching. First is my will that you should have it, and then I make you wish for it, and then I make you beseech it."*

Just as "the Spirit of the Son," making common cause with our own spirits, works in us Christ's Abba relationship with the Father, so too that same Spirit gathers and reorders the disparate dimensions of our paradoxical and contradictory selves. We then find ourselves, in the words of Saint Paul, "transformed by the renewing of [our] minds, so that [we] may discern what is the will of God" (Rom. 12:2). The Spirit who prays within us is also the Spirit of truth who, drawing from the "boundless riches" of Christ, overturns our various "idols" of how we or the church should be and, in the words of an ancient hymn, enables "with perpetual light, the dullness of our blinded sight."

This is wonderfully described by Saint Isaac of Syria, a seventh-century theologian and one of the great figures in the spiritual tradition of the Eastern Church.

> When the Spirit dwells within a person, from that moment that person has become prayer; the Spirit never leaves them. For the Spirit himself never ceases to pray within us. Whether we are asleep or awake, from then

---

* Julian of Norwich, *Showings*, chap. 19 (Short Text), trans. E. C. Colledge, OSA, and J. Walsh, SJ, Classics of Western Spirituality (Mahwah, NJ: Paulist, 1978), 157.

on prayer never departs from our soul. Whether we are eating or drinking or sleeping or whatever else we are doing, even if we are in the deepest of sleeps, the incense of prayer is rising without effort in our hearts. Prayer never deserts us. In every moment of our life, even when it appears to have ceased, prayer is secretly at work within us continually.*

It is this secret all-permeating presence of the Spirit who prays within us below the level of our consciousness that overtakes us and moves us to illumination or action or both. And because the Spirit also pours into our hearts the capacity to love out of the fullness of the love we name as God, we begin to see the world and all creation with the mercy and compassion that reflect the love with which "God so loved the world that he gave his only Son" (John 3:16).

As we yield more and more to the motions of the Spirit, the compassion of God takes root in us as our hearts are healed and rendered merciful. "And what is a merciful heart?" an elder once asked Saint Isaac. This was his reply:

It is the heart's burning for the sake of the entire creation, for men, for birds, for animals, for demons, for every created thing; and at the recollection and sight of them, the eyes of a merciful man pour forth abundant tears. From the strong and vehement mercy that grips his heart and from his great compassion, his heart is humbled and he cannot bear to hear or to see any injury or slight sorrow

---

* Quoted in *Celebrating the Seasons*, ed. Robert Atwell (Harrisburg, PA: Morehouse, 2001), 296.

in creation. For this reason he offers up prayers with tears continually even for irrational beasts, for the enemies of the truth, and for those who harm him, that they may be protected and receive mercy. And in like manner he even prays for the family of reptiles, because of the great compassion that burns without measure in his heart in the likeness of God.*

This is, of course, the description of a cosmic heart, a heart in which the Spirit of the Son has long colluded with our spirit, and produced its fruit, forming the Christ in us, and enabling us to cry, "Abba," not only in our own voice but on behalf of all creation, including the reptiles, a symbol here of all that threatens or repels us. A heart such as this is beyond anything we can create though psychological effort or active imagination: it is pure gift. Prayer opens the way, and the grace of God's goodness does the rest.

So beware, prayer can be dangerous. As we make ourselves available and give root-room to the Spirit, who prays within us, we may be taken well beyond all that we can ask or imagine. We may find ourselves, in the words of Saint John of the Cross, "on strange islands where we have never been before." To find ourselves on such strange islands can be disorienting and challenging. At the same time, we may find there an expansion of consciousness, a new way of seeing, and the courage to embrace even the reptiles in the strength of God's compassion worked into our hearts by the Spirit.

---

* *The Ascetical Homilies of St. Isaac the Syrian*, Homily 71, 2nd ed. (Boston: Holy Transfiguration Monastery, 2011), 491.

*Mark's Questions about Prayer in the Light
of God's Trinitarian Life*

As Frank's theology of prayer just above makes luminously clear, prayer is the transforming gift of God's presence. So, I would like to see if the Trinitarian theology we have explored throughout this book can help us consider some practical questions that often arise.

First, do we really need to set aside a specific time for prayer? As Frank observes, like every intimate relationship, our relationship with God calls for our conscious attention. By setting aside time for intentional awareness of the prayer that God is always communicating within us and throughout the universe, we ask God the Holy Spirit to make us ever more available to God's life at work within us. Setting aside some dedicated time for prayer is a concrete act we can take, which, like a sacrament, helps us to recognize a reality that is wonderful, mysterious, and ever present.

As for the length of time to set aside, this depends a great deal on each person's temperament and circumstance. The essential thing is to have a dedicated period of time in which you can simply hand your life over to God; an identifiable "window" of time through which you can become more consciously aware of your relationship with God. Having a dedicated time for prayer at some point during the day usually makes it easier to turn to God throughout the day.

For some people, this dedicated time may be as brief as five minutes, for others half an hour or an hour may be fulfilling. Longer time is not necessarily better and can, just as Frank noted above, become an object we have to achieve or a source of self-preoccupied frustration or satisfaction. We simply want to dedicate this time to God and to keep to this time, peacefully and nonanxiously waiting upon God. In the quiet acceptance of the divine presence we can rest, confident that God is already praying within us no matter what we may or may not experience during any given prayer time.

I have almost always found it helpful to pray with a set portion of Scripture, with periods of silence in which to ask God to speak anew the deep meaning of these words. Additionally, meditation or mindfulness exercises — such as focusing on the gentle flowing in and out of your own breath — can be a helpful means of becoming more attentive in a nonjudgmental way to your own thoughts. This is very useful because it may allow you to step back from your thoughts and simply notice them without becoming carried along by them. Each time you become aware that your mind has "wandered," you peacefully return to a phrase or word from Scripture or to an awareness of your own breathing. Becoming more deeply centered in your own body, and more aware of the various levels of thought and feeling within you, allows you to come before God more fully as yourself, the one whom God has always known and loved.

Another question that often arises is whether it makes sense, or is even right, to ask God for things in prayer. When we are moved to ask God for anything in prayer, this could *not* be a case of us helpfully informing God of something that might have escaped the divine attention. Rather, we can understand this as *God the Holy Spirit bringing to our own consciousness something that we need to talk to God about*. In other words, the question is not, does God know what we need or most deeply desire, but do we? If we come before God embarrassed about, perhaps hiding from, or even unconscious of the deepest longings and fears of our own hearts, then we place an artificial person between the truth of ourselves and God. Mercifully, because God is unalterably in love with us, God the Holy Spirit tugs and presses upon the truth of ourselves — so that it may come to the surface of our relationship with God and be received.

In time, as we learn to trust God's love for us, that love who is the Holy Spirit plumbs our hearts ever more deeply, allowing us to recognize and hold before God yet more significant aspects of ourselves. In doing so, we will find that God cherishes us so much that God continually deepens those desires — deepens them so that we may come to discover that what we desire most profoundly in all our longings is really *God*, God's love, and there is nothing God longs to give us more than this.

There is a most wonderful and unexpected aspect of all this: namely, that God seems to delight in involving us and our fellow creatures in the fulfilling of God's will. Accordingly, just as God might inspire us to share in advancing God's reign by, say, protesting against racial injustice, so God also draws us into collaboration with the divine project by inspiring us to pray for things. In other words, it pleases God that certain events should come about according to our prayer, for in this way we share with our fellow creatures in the bringing about of God's will. Moreover, sometimes when God answers our prayer in a very direct and obvious way — say, in bringing about a wonderfully beautiful day for a walk with a friend — then that particular grace (the beautiful day, for example) becomes a very real sign of almost sacramental power for us, a sign of God's love and desire to involve us in God's action within the world. Of course, *every* day is a gift to us from God, but it is God's delight that through our prayer this particular day becomes *recognizable* to us precisely as God's gift in answer to our prayer.

Another set of questions that often arises has to do with distractions in prayer, and the apparently different problem of spiritual dryness, the feeling that nothing "is happening" during our prayer time or that God is somehow absent to us. Let me try to show why in fact these are often related issues. What we experience as distractions are very likely concerns or desires of some real significance to us, which for some reason have not been able to rise to the surface of prayer, and which the Holy Spirit mercifully brings to our attention — even though we may experience this divine prompting as a distraction from our "real" prayer. So, it can often be very helpful, as you become mindful of these various concerns or wants, *not* to attempt pushing them away from your attention but rather to speak with God directly about them. You might begin simply by asking God to help you more clearly perceive and ponder these pressing thoughts, holding them and naming them before God. Sometimes I have found it very freeing just saying to God, "Well, Lord, here is this thing that I keep thinking about and I don't know what to do about it." Very often the simple act of holding your concerns before God in this way brings a powerful sense of consolation: God is with you in these concerns and accepts you lovingly with all of them roiling within you. As you talk about each of them with God, you may find a growing but often indefinable sense of clarity or direction. In this way, something that seemed to "get in the way" of prayer becomes the *subject* of our conversation with God, and open to God's healing and illumination and new life.

I think that the problem of spiritual dryness is, at least sometimes, closely related to this issue of distractions in prayer.

Once we stop trying to push away the "distracting concerns" and instead hold them openly and directly before God, we may well find that our sense of God's presence becomes much livelier and life-giving. God has been profoundly present in our prayer time, but perhaps our own authentic self has not been present to God. And this situation might well present itself as an experience of dryness in prayer or of God's seeming absence. In such possible situations, it can be very helpful to speak to God directly about our bewilderment: "Oh Lord," we might ask, "is there something I need to speak before you? Help me to entrust the whole of my being to your loving embrace."

There is also another possible way of interpreting a long season of divine silence in prayer (and a good spiritual director would be of considerable help in thinking about this possibility). Sometimes in our spiritual journey we have experienced intense moments of awareness, moments when God seemed especially close to us, perhaps communicating to us a moving sense of God's love for us. These have been, and always remain, moments of particular significance for us, moments that God uses to communicate with us, and to which we may often fruitfully return.

Yet sometimes, as Saint John of the Cross observes in his remarkable work *The Dark Night of the Soul*, our spiritual development may bring us to a season when God begins to awaken us to a deeper sense of God's presence — *a presence so beautiful and infinite that it is incomprehensible to us now*. It is not at all that God has withdrawn from us; on the contrary, God may be drawing us more wholly into the infinite reality of God's life. But we have been used to God moving more immediately with us, or identifiable signs of God's presence with us. In such a case, the absence of experience, or the darkness that we sense, is in fact very like the dazzling "darkness" that overtakes us when we gaze for a moment at the sun; the darkness or absence we experience is the only way our spiritual senses can register the overwhelming and infinitely loving presence of God.

The final set of questions I want to consider relates to the issue of seemingly unanswered prayer. Here it will be helpful to reflect on the prayerful nature of Jesus's relation to the Father. Christ made of his entire life and his death an offering of prayer, and the Father's answer was expressed in our world as the resurrection of Christ. In a very real sense, our prayer is always a sharing into this fundamental prayer relationship, the presence in our broken world of the infinitely generous self-communication of God the Trinity.

So, when we ask for things in prayer, we are not simply coming before the creator as one creature, but rather we are adopted in Christ as God's beloved children who bring our needs and fears and hopes to the One whom Christ loved. Thus, by God's grace, what we pray for is always caught up within the relationship of Jesus to the Father in their Holy Spirit. And this means that there is never an unanswered prayer, for our prayer is simply our sharing into the inexhaustible self-sharing life of the Trinity. But even if we grant this intellectually, how does it help us with our feeling that sometimes there is no "answer" to our prayer that we can recognize?

It helps us in this way, I believe. By trusting that our prayer is caught up within the infinite life of God — and indeed, that "our" prayer flows from this divine life — we begin to realize that the real "answer" of God to any prayer is nothing less than God's infinite life. Prayer is our share in God giving God to God, the Trinity, and therefore the beautiful day we pray for, or the health of a friend, is always answered by God with the outpouring of God's own life and never-failing love. Sometimes God manifests this infinite outpouring within a finite form that we can perceive, for example, by means of a particular fine day or a particular return to health for which we have prayed. But at other times God responds to our prayer in a way that surpasses anything we can now perceive, for God is giving Godself.

As strange as it may seem, sometimes what *we* genuinely *want* to ask God for is something a great deal less than the infinite life and love of God. And thus God's response may be imperceptible to us, too immense for us to grasp. The paradigm case that helps us to sense this reality in our own lives is the prayer of Jesus in Gethsemane — a prayer that the One who loves Jesus did in fact answer, not by removing human suffering and death from Jesus's path, but by making present within our world the infinite and inexhaustible life of God, manifest as the resurrection of Jesus from the dead. Over the years of our prayer, we may ask God the Holy Spirit to work ever more fully within us our sharing through baptism in Christ's dying and rising. In that way, I believe, God will indeed help us to sense the infinite and incomprehensible love and beauty and goodness of God giving God to God — that is, to sense the life of the Trinity, which is the answer to all prayers.

~~~~~~~~~~ 13 ~~~~~~~~~~

Death and the Life to Come

Frank's Thoughts on Our Death and Our Membership in Christ's Body

In thinking about death and the life to come that awaits us once we have passed through the narrow door between what we have known as life and a new mode of being, I am reminded of a conversation I had with a close friend who was dying of brain cancer. He was a monk and a person of deep prayer, so I had no reluctance in asking him directly, "How do you feel about dying?" He paused for a moment and then replied, "I feel scared because I don't know what it will be like, but I am also curious." I appreciated his honesty, and, reflecting later on what he had said, I realized that he had brought to my awareness my own unacknowledged thoughts about death and the afterlife: fear of the unknown and also curiosity. For Saint Paul, who longed to be with Christ, death signaled the fulfillment: "Then I will know fully, even as I have been fully known" (1 Cor. 13:12), and entering into a new state of being.

"We will not all die," he tells us, "but we will all be changed. . . . For this perishable body must put on imperishability, and this mortal body must put on immortality" (1 Cor. 15:50–53).

As limbs of Christ's body, we are caught up with Christ into the resurrection. "Sleeper, awake! Rise from the dead, and Christ will shine on you." This summons from the Letter to the Ephesians, which is possibly also a fragment of an early Christian hymn, appears on the lips of the risen Christ in an early Easter homily. In it Christ addresses Adam and Eve, who are captive in hell. He takes Adam by the hand and raises him up, saying, "Awake, O sleeper, and rise from the dead and Christ will give you light. . . . Rise up, work of my hands, you who were created in my image, for you are in me and I am in you; together we form only one person and we cannot be separated . . . the eternal dwelling places are prepared, the treasure houses of all good things lie open. The kingdom of heaven has been prepared for you from all eternity." Pondering these words, I am drawn to the Easter icon of Christ standing upon the battered-down doors of hell, his hands extended not in a friendly handshake, but grasping Adam and Eve by their wrists, pulling them forcibly out of their constricting tombs into the force field of resurrection life. Such is the fierce and insistent love of the risen One that knows no boundaries. "I am convinced, " writes Paul, "that neither death, nor life, nor angels, nor rulers, nor things present, nor things to come, nor powers, nor height, nor depth, nor anything else in all creation, will be able to separate us from the love of God in Jesus Christ our Lord" (Rom. 8:38–39).

So it is that in leaving this life and passing through death, we are drawn forward by the deathless love that lies at the heart of the universe and sustains all things in being; the love that

is the very life of the Trinity, as Mark has so wonderfully reminded us in the ongoing flow of our reflections. Death opens
the way for a further unfolding of the mystery of God's Trinitarian self-sharing as goodness and love in which we live and
move and have our being.

The life to come is a "passover" from one dimension of love
into another. Like my friend, I am scared but curious about
what lies ahead and find I am drawn to the notion of a further unfolding of my life in relation to God's self-gift, which
brought me into being and will sustain me on the other side
of death. As he came to his final days, my friend was asked
if he wanted to go to hospice. Without hesitation he replied
emphatically, "No, I want to go to heaven."

The understanding that "what we shall be has yet to be
revealed" (1 John 3:2), together with the white stone in Revelation 2:17 on which is written my new name, suggests that living
into the full mystery of who I am in grace and truth occurs on
the other side of what we call death. At the same time, my new
name is the revelation of how God in Christ knows and loves
me: I will then know myself as I am known by God, beyond all
efforts at self-construction, or assessment.

With a strong conviction of the life that awaits us beyond
this life, the early church spoke of one's death day as one's *Dies
Natalis*, one's birthday into eternity, signaling a new stage of
being and becoming. Life when we die is not taken away: it is
changed, transfigured by God's all-embracing love, the same
love that drew Jesus through death into resurrection. What we
know of life — the gathering up of all that we have lived from
the day of our birth — is then fitted into a larger frame called
eternity, which is not a place but an ever-present dimension of
reality that surrounds us and impinges upon us. So, we don't so

much die *out* of life as we die *into* life — life yet to be revealed beyond all imagining, of which love is the source — "For the steadfast love of the Lord never ceases."

Being born into eternity, rather than signifying "rest in peace," which we pray will be afforded to the departed, inaugurates a new dimension of life. If it is a season of peace, then it is a peace "which passes all understanding" because it is of a totally new order. Saint John of the Cross speaks of the experience of God as finding ourselves on "strange islands" where we have never before been. Such, I imagine, is the experience that awaits us when we die. It is impossible, however, to imagine what it will be like, since we are limited to our experience of time and space. Eternity is beyond our concepts of time and duration, just as God is beyond any concepts or images we may have of God. "God does not offer himself to our finite beings as a thing all complete and ready to be embraced. For us, God is eternal discovery and eternal growth."* These are the words of Pierre Teilhard de Chardin, the Jesuit paleontologist for whom evolution was a sign of God's active presence in the cosmos.

In a passage from the Gospel of John, which is frequently read at funerals, Jesus tells his disconsolate disciples that he is soon to leave them and that his hour of glorification has arrived. By way of encouragement, he tells them not to let their hearts be troubled: "Believe in God, believe also in me. In my Father's house there are many dwelling places. If it were not so, would I have told you that I go to prepare a place for you?" (John 14:1–2). Jesus is, of course, speaking metaphorically

---

* Quoted in Louis M. Savary, *The Divine Milieu Explained* (Mahwah, NJ: Paulist, 2004), 226.

about what awaits his followers after they have died and been taken by him to the Father's house. Note that the word for "dwelling places" can be used to describe "resting places" such as might be found along a caravan route. This possible meaning did not escape early commentators, who saw such resting places as stages in an ongoing journey of spiritual growth and discovery on the other side of death. From this perspective, "growing up in all ways into Christ" continues after death. And Christ's risen body, of which we are declared members through baptism, continues "building itself up in love."

A prayer for the departed in the Book of Common Prayer asks that the person who has died, "increasing in knowledge and love of thee . . . may go from strength to strength in the life of perfect service in thy heavenly kingdom." Moving more deeply into the deathless life and love of the Trinity, which is to move more deeply into the mystery of who I am and am called to be, involves knowledge and love, and here we encounter judgment: who have we been and what do we bring with us into this new dimension of life; what needs to be forgiven or healed or let go in order for us to go from strength to strength? Saint John of the Cross tells us, "In the evening of life we will be judged on love alone." As I read and reflect upon these words, several phrases from Scripture come to mind:

> With you is the fountain of life;
> in your light we see light (Ps. 36:9),

and "For now we see in a mirror, dimly, but then we will see face to face. . . . Then I will know fully, even as I have been fully known" (1 Cor. 13:12). When we die, I believe we are drawn by Christ into the fuller presence of the Trinity, and in the light of that goodness and love that pass all understanding and overleap anything we can imagine, we see light; that is, we see ourselves as we truly are; we are overwhelmed, and, like Job, all we can do is fall down and cry,

> "I had heard of you by the hearing of the ear,
> but now my eye sees you;
> therefore I despise myself,
> and repent in dust and ashes." (Job 42:5–6)

This is not a cry of self-castigation; rather, it expresses how we see with the eyes of faith the truth of who we are as God knows and loves us: "Then I will know as I am fully known." Judgment, forgiveness, and reconciliation are all one as we come home to ourselves as "Beloved," which is to know ourselves as we are known by God. Hell, which is ours to choose, is to keep our eyes tightly shut and refuse to see "face to face." Hell can also be the refusal to accept forgiveness and therefore resist the grasp of the risen Christ, who welcomes us to the kingdom of heaven, which has been prepared for us "from all eternity." In other words, hell is not a state imposed upon us by God but a condition we impose upon ourselves.

As I grow older, and death draws closer, eternity becomes more and more my frame of reference. When life as I know it ends, everything within it will be gathered up and fitted into eternity along with all other lives. Here is where all spatial and temporal categories fail. Eternity is totally other, yet completely real in a way that is beyond all comprehension. When I try to imagine what it will be like, I am quickly checked and at the same time consoled by God's words to Isaiah,

For my thoughts are not your thoughts,
    nor are your way my ways, says the LORD.
For as the heavens are higher than the earth,
    so are my ways higher than your ways,
    and my thoughts than your thoughts.

(Isa. 55:8–9)

Eternity is finding our true home beyond death within the eternal mystery of love and goodness we name as the Trinity.

As I look ahead to my own dying, I find myself in a state of awe and expectation and, yes, some anxiety: what will it be like? I am also drawn to a prayer of Teilhard de Chardin that has become very much my own.

> After having perceived you [O God] as he who is "a greater myself" grant, when my hour comes, that I may recognize you under the species of each alien or hostile force that seems bent upon destroying or uprooting me. When the signs of age begin to mark my body (and still more when they touch my mind); when the ill that is to diminish me or carry me off strikes from without or is born within me; when the painful fact that I am losing hold of myself and am absolutely passive within the hands of the great unknown forces that have formed me; in all those dark moments, O God, grant that I may understand that it is you (provided only that my faith is strong enough) who are painfully parting the fibers of my being in order to penetrate to the very marrow of my substance and bear me away within yourself.*

* Pierre Teilhard de Chardin, *The Divine Milieu* (New York: Perennial Classics, 1960), 56–57.

*Mark's Thoughts on the Journey from Life among God's Gifts
into the Life of the Giver*

I want to reflect on one passage that, for me, expresses the very
heart of what Frank has been saying — and which is particularly meaningful to me, as ALS has brought to stillness and
silence much of who I was. Frank writes, "When we die, I believe we are drawn by Christ into the fuller presence of the
Trinity, and in the light of that goodness and love that pass all
understanding and overleap anything we can imagine, we see
light; that is, we see ourselves as we truly are." Frank also men-
tions the "white stone" (described in the book of Revelation)
on which is written our true name, our true identity as God has
eternally known and loved us.

Whenever we face death, whether our own or that of those
we love, we are inevitably overwhelmed by our sense of loss
and separation from all that gives our lives meaning. These
feelings are right and natural — Jesus himself wept at the death
of his friend Lazarus. The earthly joys and relationships, the
stories and adventures we've shared together, the struggles and
heartbreaks we have learned gradually to accept (and sometimes overcome), the wonders we have imagined and built
together — all these seem to vanish into the darkness of death.
So, our grief is profoundly natural and flows from our love of
all that has been.

And yet we believe that at the heart of the natural goodness
we have known, and which we mourn, there is a hidden or
mystical reality. For all the goodness and joy and love we have
experienced in earthly things are an echo of heaven, and an
invitation. In the words of Thomas Traherne, "The Sun is but
a little spark of His infinite love: the Sea is but one drop of His

goodness. But what flames of love ought that spark to kindle in your soul: what seas of affection ought to flow for that drop in your bosom!"* Already in this life we have begun to taste the infinite goodness of God, and, Traherne hopes, this "little spark of his infinite love" will awaken us to our true destiny in God. Few mystical theologians capture more graciously than Traherne this sense that God's overwhelming generosity to us, even now in our mortal life, has the power to open our minds and hearts to the great Giver of all these gifts — and so help us by means of this contemplation to begin right now to live in the heart of God:

> You never enjoy the world aright, till you see how a sand exhibiteth the wisdom and power of God: And prize in everything the service which they do you, by manifesting His glory and goodness to your soul. You never enjoy the world aright, till the Sea itself floweth in your veins, till you are clothed with the heavens, and crowned with the stars. Your enjoyment of the world is never right, till every morning you awake in Heaven; see yourself in your Father's Palace; and look upon the skies, the earth, and the air as Celestial Joys: having such a reverend esteem of all, as if you were among the Angels.†

To experience this world as we should, and to understand what it foretells for us, we should revel and rejoice in the astonishingly generous beauty of God's creation; we should, says

---

* Thomas Traherne, *Centuries* 2.14, ed. H. M. Margoliouth (Oxford: Clarendon, 1958), 62–63 (spelling modified).
† Traherne, *Centuries* 1.27–29, pp. 14–15.

Traherne, begin to realize how much God longs to share the life of heaven with us, "till the Sea itself floweth in your veins, till you are clothed with the heavens, and crowned with the stars." And perhaps by contemplating our present existence in this way, we shall even now awaken every morning in heaven, for we shall begin to realize how much of the heavenly life God has already clothed and crowned us with in this life.

This helps me to think about our belief that at death our life is changed but not ended, because the life we have lived in this world has a source over which death has no dominion. For the life of this world continually flows to us from God's inexhaustible life. Right now it comes to us through the finite, mortal stuff of this earth — our physical biology, the molecular composition and physics of each ocean wave, the neuropsychology of a baby's first smile, the breathtaking imagination of a poet's art. These good and wonderful channels of God's infinite generosity, as treasurable and irreplaceable as they are, still are only mortal. And the fact that they must all come to an end in their own time draws us to the mystical wellspring at the heart of them all — the deathless life of God.

The journey from our earthly life into the very source and heart of all life in God is a journey God alone can make possible. For me, this is what Frank means when he says that Christ brings us into the fuller presence of the Trinity, into the fuller presence of that infinite self-sharing that has secretly been the very ground of our earthly existence. In Christ we will share, without any mediation of mortal structures, directly in the inexhaustible life who is God; God will simply be the life we lead.

Perhaps most mysteriously to us, God seems to have created a universe in which we beloved creatures are only able fully to discover our true selves, our true names, by giving ourselves away in love and freedom to each other — and ultimately by handing over our mortal life itself. And yet, of course, we know this is the very rhythm and heart of God's own Trinitarian life, a life in which each of the divine persons *is* delighted by an endless giving to each other. And we have been known and cherished eternally within that endless generosity. From that divine life we have drawn our life on earth, and within that divine life we shall finally know ourselves and be set free to become ourselves in truth.

The Communion of Saints and Mary

FRANK T. GRISWOLD

The Friendship of Saints as a Channel of God's Love

Several years ago, while teaching a course on liturgy at a theological seminary, I was commenting on the Apostles' Creed,
which was recited daily in the chapel in the course of Morning
and Evening Prayer. I asked the twenty-five men and women
before me: "What do we mean when we say: 'I believe in the
communion of saints'?" Dead silence. Some looked toward
the ceiling while other typed away furiously on their lap-
tops searching for an answer. I waited. Finally, in a timid and
somewhat questioning voice, a seminarian replied: "A cloud
of witnesses?"

I knew at that moment there was work to do! When, following Saint Paul, we declare that the church is the body of
Christ, of which we are acknowledged as limbs and members
in baptism, it is important to remember that we continue to
be limbs and members of Christ's body as we make the transition from life as we know it to life as it has yet to be revealed.

It is the risen Christ, who, in the power of the Spirit, draws us through death into a new mode of being illumined by the light of the resurrection and sustained by Christ's deathless love. The communion of saints is the church's affirmation of our continuing relation to those who have passed beyond this life and are growing into the fullness of who they are as God's beloved, and as such, knowing "fully," as they have been "fully known" (1 Cor.13:12).

In her *Revelations of Divine Love*, Julian of Norwich tells us, "The purpose of God's revelation to me was to teach our soul the wisdom of cleaving to the goodness of God." Then, beginning with the incarnation, she goes on to reflect upon examples of God's incalculable love, and the "helps" that manifest God's goodness. Among them is the communion of saints. "Similarly," she writes, "the help that comes from particular saints and the blessed company of heaven, the delightful love and eternal fellowship we enjoy with them are due to his goodness. For through his goodness God has ordained the means to help us both glorious and many."*

What is important here is that the saints and the blessed company of heaven — limbs of Christ's risen body — and the "help" they offer us do not originate with them but have their origin in God's goodness. Evelyn Underhill once observed that it is only through God and the gift of God's grace that the saints can "help" us. For example, to ask Saint Francis to help me have a greater reverence and care for creation is to ask for him to pray to God for the grace that I may so do. In addition, just as I might ask a friend I respect to companion me with support

---

* Julian of Norwich, quoted in *Celebrating the Seasons*, ed. Robert Atwell (Harrisburg, PA: Morehouse, 2001), Thursday after Trinity 11.

in a particular situation, so too I can ask for companionship and support from a particular saint or beloved member of the "blessed company of heaven." When we proclaim, "I believe in the communion of saints," we are acknowledging that we are supported and sustained by a vast fellowship of love and prayer. The men and women who have gone before us and passed through the door of death continue to be present with us.

We often think of saints as those who have been officially acknowledged by the church for their exemplary lives. However, participation in the communion of saints is not reserved for those who have been formally declared saints by the church or commemorated in the church's calendar. In the New Testament the term "saint" is broadly applied to all who belong to the community of faith. A family member, a teacher, a friend, the companion of one's heart may have touched our lives in such a way that they continue beyond death to be a companion, an inspiration, a guide. The Holy Spirit, who is the minister of communion, binds us together in a relationship that remains unbroken by death. From time to time, the veil between us is pierced, sometimes in very surprising ways. As a pastor, I have witnessed many instances when the boundary between life and death as we know it has been breached.

For example, following his wife's funeral, a grieving husband, in the company of his daughter, hears a broken radio in the basement playing the song that was "theirs" when they were courting. They rush to the basement, and the radio, which wasn't plugged in, stops. "It's just like her," the husband exclaims, knowing in that instant that "love is stronger than death."

Several years after the death of his father due to alcoholism, a son who had left his father's grave unmarked because of his continuing anger, was visited by his father in a dream. "I did the best I could," his father sorrowfully told him. The son woke in a surge of compassion, and the anger was dissipated. The next day he ordered a gravestone.

I could go on, and I have no doubt that "explanations" can be offered for such happenings. If, however, the communion of saints is, as described in the Book of Common Prayer, a "fellowship of love and prayer" that surrounds and supports us, such in-breakings can be expected and welcomed.

I think here of Simone Weil's "chance encounter" with George Herbert's poem "Love (III)," which she found in a book loaned to her while she was on retreat at the French Benedictine Abbey of Solesmes. (This poem is included in chapter 2.) She writes that as she recited what she simply thought was a beautiful poem, "Christ himself came down and took possession of me." The "help" in this case was the witness of George Herbert through his poem that conveyed his own encounter with Christ to a searching soul on this side of death. So it is that the lives and the writings of those who have gone before us can confirm, encourage, illumine, and stretch us. They find their way into our lives at just the moment we are ready to receive their lived wisdom and companionship. This is one of the ways our forebears in faith still speak to us and serve as guides and companions.

Though such "helps," as Julian tells us, come from God, they are delivered by someone in the communion of saints: an ordinary person or a formally proclaimed saint. We might ask ourselves if we are disposed to receive such "helps." The following prayer, from the Scottish Episcopal Church, might serve to open us to a more robust sense of the communion of saints, and the enduring bond of love and prayer that ties us together:

O God, the King of saints, we praise and glorify your holy
Name for all your servants who have finished their course
in your faith and fear: for the blessed Virgin Mary; for the
holy patriarchs, prophets, apostles, and martyrs; and for
all your other righteous servants, known to us and unknown; and we pray that, encouraged by their examples,
aided by their prayers, and strengthened by their fellowship, we also may be partakers of the inheritance of the
saints in light; through the merits of your Son Jesus Christ
our Lord. Amen.

Mary, Agent in the Mystery of Salvation

This prayer gives particular recognition in the communion
of saints to Mary, the Mother of Jesus, as do many prayers of
churches in both East and West. By virtue of her unique role
in the incarnation, Mary has occupied a special place in the
liturgical and devotional life of Christians across the ages. Her
response to Gabriel's announcement that she was to conceive
and bear the Son of the Most High: "Here am I, the servant of
the Lord; let it be with me according to your word," makes her
the example of faithful availability to God's call, as demanding and mysterious as it might be. Luke tells us that Mary was
"deeply disturbed" by the angel's greeting. In response, Gabriel
urges her, "Do not be afraid, Mary, for you have found favor
with God." Likewise, what "life" may set before us as a call can
"deeply disturb" us by its magnitude and seeming impossibil-
ity and, like Mary's, come at a cost that demands everything.
What a mercy it is that Gabriel, before he departs, informs
Mary that her kinswoman Elizabeth, who was barren, is now

six months pregnant, adding as he does so, "For God, nothing will be impossible." Mary's response is to go "with haste" to visit her. Is her haste occasioned by her urgent need to have the consolation of another human being caught up into the wildness of God's ways — someone she knows — with whom she can share what has just occurred?

Upon Mary's arrival, Elizabeth's child leaps in her womb, and Elizabeth, moved by the Holy Spirit, confirms Gabriel's annunciation as she cries out, "Blessed are you among women, and blessed is the fruit of your womb." This fully human word, uttered by a kinswoman, is a second annunciation. And it is at this point that Mary bursts into song:

> "My soul magnifies the Lord,
>   and my spirit rejoices in God my Savior,
> for he has looked with favor on the lowliness of
>   his servant.
>   Surely, from now on all generations will call
>   me blessed." (Luke 1:46–48)

It would seem that Mary needed a confirming word from someone she trusted, just as we may need a confirming word from someone else before *we* too can fully embrace and rejoice in what presents itself as God's call.

Though Scripture says little about Mary, she does appear at various moments in the Gospels and most dramatically is found standing at the foot of the cross as Simeon's prophecy, that "a sword will pierce your own soul too," is fulfilled. As a mother, she must have undergone an interior death as her beloved son cried out, "It is finished." Then, following the resurrection, we find her with the disciples at prayer on the

eve of Pentecost. Had she who had died with her son also in-
wardly risen with him? Looking back over her life as one who
pondered and treasured what she heard and experienced, had
Zechariah's prophecy hovered over her at various moments?
Had Mary sensed the sword's presence when Jesus as a boy
lingered behind in the temple and was thought to be lost;
when he disappeared for forty days into the wilderness; when
he incurred the wrath of the synagogue in Nazareth, and the
hostility of the religious establishment in Jerusalem; when she
went to restrain him because people were saying, "He has gone
out of his mind" (Mark 3:21)? As her life and that of her son
unfolded, her "Let it be with me according to your word" had
to be uttered over and over, and probably in tension with the
question she had posed to Gabriel, "How can this be?" When
the sword finally did its brutal work as she stood at the foot of
the cross, was there, in the horror of it, also a sense of relief that
nothing more or worse could happen?

Mary's journey from the descent of the Holy Spirit upon
her in Nazareth to the outpouring of the Spirit at Pentecost
reveals her to be the figure of faithful availability to God's ways,
as beyond reason and demanding as they may be, and as one
who knows in the depth of her being the cost of discipleship.
Standing, therefore, with hands uplifted in prayer, as she does
in many icons and mosaics, she is the image of the church, attentive and receptive to the Spirit, as its members "grow up in
every way into him who is the head, into Christ" (Eph. 4:15).

Mary's role in the mystery of the incarnation, as recorded
in the Gospels, opened the way early on for her becoming a
focus of attention for Irenaeus (c. 130–c. 200) and other early
theologians who sought to determine the boundaries of or-
thodoxy in a sea of competing and passionately held views

concerning the nature of God and the person of Christ. In his treatise *Against Heresies*, Irenaeus draws the contrast between the disobedience of Eve, our foremother, and the obedience of Mary. As one virgin's action led to condemnation, so the fiat of another virgin led to salvation.

This same association with Eve is made by Gabriel in a homily by a fourth-century bishop, Antipater of Bostra: "You have acquired the grace that the first woman lost. She alone, yielded to the tempter's guile," the angel informs Mary. "Now you alone, are bearing the conqueror of temptation. You will bring forth a son and shall name him Jesus."*

We can see in these examples — and there are many others — that Mary, though still the humble servant of the Lord, had early on acquired a cosmic significance in relation to her role in the mystery of salvation. In one of his sermons, Bernard of Clairvaux addresses Mary as she pondered her response to Gabriel, "On your lips hangs . . . the salvation of all the sons and daughters of Adam, your entire race. Give your answer quickly, my Virgin. My Lady, speak the word that earth and hell, and heaven itself are waiting for."†

Mary, understood as the new Eve in parallel with Paul's designation of Jesus as the "last Adam" and the "second man," was captured in Latin, in which "Eva" with letters reversed became "Ave," the first word of Gabriel's greeting.

Because Scripture tells us nothing of Mary's life prior to Gabriel's appearance in Luke, and the statement in Matthew

---

* Antipater of Bostra, quoted in *Drinking from the Hidden Fountain: A Patristic Breviary*, ed. Thomas Spidlik (Kalamazoo, MI: Cistercian Publications, 1994), 394.

† Bernard of Clairvaux, quoted in *Celebrating the Seasons*, ed. Robert Atwell (Harrisburg, PA: Morehouse, 2001), 36.

that she was engaged to Joseph, but before they lived together, "she was found to be with child from the Holy Spirit," there was interest, early on, in Mary's prior life, and what had prepared her for her unique vocation. The noncanonical Infancy Gospel of James, written around the middle of the second century, met that need. It chronicles Mary's miraculous birth to a childless couple, Joachim and Anna, her purity and holiness of life, together with an expansion of the accounts of the annunciation and the role of Joseph as found in the canonical Gospels. Mary's presentation in the temple and other events drawn from this noncanonical source are reflected primarily in the iconography and liturgy of the churches of the East and, to a lesser degree, the West.

A prayer from the third or fourth century, known in the West as *Sub Tuum Presidium*, bears witness to the importance of Mary in the life and prayer of the early church, and is still in use, particularly in churches of the East.

> Beneath your compassion,
> we take refuge, O Theotokos:
> Do not despise our petitions in time of trouble,
> but rescue us from dangers
> only pure, only blessed one.

To this day, this prayer, in slightly different forms, is widely used in churches both in the East and in the West. It is the earliest reference we have to Mary as *Theotokos* (God-bearer), a title affirmed at the Council of Ephesus in 431, and again at the Council of Chalcedon in 451. The title sought to preserve the integrity of the incarnation and of Jesus being both fully human and fully divine. Over time it opened the way for the increasing prominence of Mary in the imagination and prayer of the church, and the perception of her as a maternal refuge in the midst of the vagaries and distresses of life.

By the time of the Reformation, in many quarters in the West, devotion to Mary had displaced devotion to her Son: he was the judge and she was the compassionate intercessor on our behalf. Lest Christ's role as savior and mediator be overshadowed by her, the corrective was almost total suppression of the one who had said, "Surely, from now on all generations will call me blessed."

With reform in Marian devotion in the Roman Catholic Church and a renewed sense of the immediacy of the communion of saints, Anglican and other churches of the Reformation have begun to accord Mary a greater prominence in their worship and acknowledgment of her agency in the mystery of salvation. She is seen not only as God's humble and willing servant and a loving mother, but also as one who can withstand suffering and, as *Mater Dolorosa*, as a companion to those bearing the pain of loss. She is also a woman of courage. Her song, as recorded in the Gospel of Luke (1:46–55), known as the Magnificat, is a cry of thanksgiving from a woman self-described as "lowly" being "lifted up" and imbued with courage and boldness: "for the Mighty one has done great things for me, and holy is his name." As well, it is proclamation of prophetic judgment:

> "He has shown the strength of his arm;
> > he has scattered the proud in the thoughts of
> > > their hearts.
> He has brought down the powerful from
> > their thrones,
> > and lifted up the lowly;
> he has filled the hungry with good things,
> > and sent the rich away empty."

With such words, traditionally sung at Evening Prayer, Mary challenges us with a vision that overturns might and power, and favors the lowly, the hungry, and those who are oppressed and dispossessed.

Because the Bible includes little about her life, Mary is able to find shelter in the hearts and minds and prayers of a vast array of people across different traditions. Her recorded appearances are mostly to children and to those who are poor, and the places she chooses for such encounters are as unexceptional as Nazareth was to Nathaniel in the Gospel of John when he exclaimed, "Can anything good come out of Nazareth?" When she appears in a person's dream or finds her way into a time of contemplation, she often points to her Son and says, as she did to the servants at the wedding in Cana: "Do what he tells you."

Mary can be very much a stealth figure who shows up unannounced and when least expected. People with no prior consciousness of or draw to Mary are often startled and unsettled when she appears in their thoughts or their prayers. Sometimes they are embarrassed not only by her presence but also by her familial and intimate way with them. She doesn't seem august or as though she just stepped out of a Christmas card. Offering a word of encouragement or directing us to her son is the usual way those who have had such encounters experience her. Here I think of the Celtic tradition in which Mary is very much part of domestic life, present at milking time, or when the fire is tended, or invoked at bedtime as one shuts one's eyes: "this Who are those watching over my sleep? / The fair loving Mary and her Lamb." What could be a more consoling and intimate awareness as one drifts off into slumber than to be watched over by Mary and Jesus? A good friend who grew up with little thought of Mary beyond a childhood Christmas pageant told me she thinks of Mary as a mother who, after you have fallen asleep, creeps into your room and gently adjusts the covers to make sure that all is well before she tiptoes out again and shuts the door — a lovely "Celtic" image.

The familiar hymn "Ye Watchers and Ye Holy Ones," which is found in a number of denominational hymnals, sings of Mary with words drawn in part from a hymn of the Eastern Church in honor of the *Theotokos*:

> O higher than the cherubim,
> more glorious than the seraphim,
> lead their praises, Alleluia!
> Thou bearer of th' eternal Word,
> most gracious, magnify the Lord, Alleluia!

Mary here is very far removed from tending the fire or tucking us in at bedtime, yet within the "cloud of witnesses," that enduring fellowship of love and prayer that surrounds and supports us, which we call the communion of saints, Mary is both high and lowly as she continues to "lead their praises." Yet, "When we pray for the love of the sweet mother who bore him," Julian reminds us that the "help" she and all other saints give us "is due to God's goodness." And it is out of that divine goodness that we are united in love and prayer with those who have gone before us.

Index of Subjects

"Abba," God as, 50, 79, 80, 104, 147
Abbey of Solesmes, 169
Abraham, 22–23, 49, 85
Aelred of Rievaulx, xi, 39
Against Heresies (Irenaeus), 173
alienation from God, 45–46
ALS, author's experience of, vii, viii, xi, 11, 162
Ambrose, Saint, 135
analogies in theology, 10–16
Ananias, 125–26
Anna (Mary's mother), 174
Antipater of Bostra, 173
Apostles' Creed, 166
Augustine, Saint: and body of Christ, 137; on creation, 52; God's knowledge of humanity, 61; on prayer, 141; restlessness of, 1, 28, 79
author, analogy of God as, 7–10, 12–16, 21–22, 24, 52–53, 87

authority, 9
awareness, 8

baptism, 39, 107, 128–29, 133, 134
Benedict, Saint, x
Benedictine communities, x
Benedict's Rule for Monks, 91
Benson, Richard Meux, 137
Bernard of Clairvaux, 173
Bible, 149
Book of Common Prayer, 122, 159, 169
Brothers Karamazov, The (Dosto-yevsky), 129

Camus, Albert, 109
Catherine of Siena, Saint, 103, 141
Celtic tradition of Mary, 176–77
Chalcedon, Council of, 174
Christ. *See* Jesus
church: as body of Christ, 121,

166–67; as sacred mystery,
121–27; Saint Paul's vision of,
as body of Christ, 123, 125,
126, 128–30
Clement of Alexandria, 133
Cloud of Unknowing, The, 141
communication, God's with us,
16–20
communion, 130–31, 166–70.
See also Eucharist
contemplation, 70
creation: analogy with resurrection, 85–86; as continuous
activity, 51–53; Frank's reflection on, 58–61; God's gift
of existence, 51–54; as God's
self-expression, 59; humanity's contemplative calling,
54–58; mystery of, 51–52, 53;
and natural suffering, 61–62
crucifixion, 83–85
Cyril of Jerusalem, 132

Damascus, road to, 124–26
Dark Night of the Soul, The, 152
death: as birth into eternity,
157–58; fear of, 101–2, 155–56;
Frank's reflections on, 155–61;
as journey, 162–65
devil, 105. *See also* Satan
Dies Natalis, 157
divine life contrasted with
human life, 74, 76, 86
divinization, 97
doctrines, Christian church,
2–3
Dostoyevsky, Fyodor, 129
"Dream of the Rood, The"
105–6

Eliot, T. S., 134
Elizabeth (Mary's cousin),
170–71
Ephesus, Council of, 174
Eucharist, 135–37. *See also*
communion
evil: God's response to, 66–67;
human, mystery of, 64–65;
problem of, 61–62
evolution, 58–59

faith: dimensions of, 25–27;
Frank's reflections on, 27–30;
as God's friendship, 21–23;
and search for understanding,
30–31; as theological virtue,
25
Farrer, Austin, 58
Father Damasus, 94
fear: as antagonist of faith,
21; of death, 101–2, 155–56;
Frank's reflections on, 27–30
forgiveness and grace, 114–17
Francis of Assisi, Saint: Christ's
call, 103–4; God's beauty and
goodness, 55–56; Spirit of the
Lord, 139; spiritual freedom,
60
Frank's reflections: on death,
155–61; on faith and fear, 27–
30; on full stature of Christ,
78–80; on God's authorship,
8–10; on goodness of creation,
58–61; on grace and forgiveness, 114–17; on Jesus's death
and resurrection, 91–95; on
prayer, 139–47; on revelation, 39–40; on solidarity in
suffering, 69–71; on Trinity

and personal transformation, 48–50

freedom, 79–80

friendship: deep, 39–40; divine, 2; with God, 21–25, 36–38, 39; with Jesus, 36; of saints, 166–70; spiritual, xi

fruit of the Spirit, 79–80

Gabriel, 170–71

Garden of Eden, 101

Gelasian Sacramentary, 121

Genesis, creation stories in, 35, 58–59

Gethsemane, Jesus in garden of, 104, 154

gifts of the Spirit, 127–38

God: alienation from, 45–46; analogy of, as author, 7–10, 12–16, 21–22, 24, 52–53, 87; communication of, with us, 16–20, 32–33; friendship with, 36–38, 39; identity of, 33–36; as infinite self-giving, 41–42; intimacy with, 7–10; life of, and man's true life, 47–48; life of, as Word become flesh, 35–36; as love, 46–47, 64, 69; love and author's dog anecdote, 17–19; omnipresence of, 38–39; response of, to evil, 66–67; as self-giving love, 98; transforming presence in suffering, 65–67; and Trinity, 44–45; voice of, 32–33

Good Friday Liturgy, 122

grace: and abundant life, 111–12; characteristics of, 112–14; development of, over time,

136; as forgiveness, 114–17; and Trinity, 117–20

Great Schism (1054), 121

Gregory of Nazianzus, 48–49, 133

Gregory the Great, 69–70

Griswold, Frank T. *See* Frank's reflections

Harvest of Hope (McIntosh and Griswold), 20, 81

hearts, merciful and cosmic, 146–47

heaven, 158–60, 164

hell, 160

Herbert, George, 29–30, 109, 143, 169

Holy Spirit: and resurrection, 88; and self-identity, 43–45

hope, 5, 25

Hopkins, Gerard Manley, 59–60, 132

idols, 34, 37

Ignatius of Loyola, Saint, x, 115, 132, 142

intimacy with God, 7–10

Irenaeus, Saint, 135–36, 172–73

Isaac, 134

Isaac of Syria, Saint, 145–47

Israel, 32–35

Jesuit communities, x

Jesus: awakening to Christ, 80–81; crucifixion of, 83–85; divine life of, contrasted with human life, 74, 76, 86; Frank's reflections on full stature of Christ, 78–80; friendship with, 36, 82–83; identity of,

73–76; passion of, 82–83;
patterns of relationships, 73,
75–76; resurrection of, 85–88;
risen Christ, 88–90; stories
of, 72–73, 76–77; time with,
76–78; and withdrawal for
prayer, 104–5
Joachim (Mary's father), 174
John of the Cross, Saint, 119,
147, 152, 158, 159
Julian of Norwich: communion
of saints, 169, 177; friendship with Jesus, 40; mystical
encounters, 145; on prayer,
140; *Revelations of Divine Love*,
167; on sin and God's love, 99,
108, 115–16

Lazarus, 162
L'Engle, Madeleine, 10
Leo the Great, 135
Lewis, C. S., 4
life journeys, 91–93
living water, 1
Logos, 131
love: and gifts of the Spirit,
127–38; as God's self-gift,
126–27; infinite, God as,
46–47; love's story of salvation, 100–103; as theological
virtue, 25
"Love (III)" (Herbert), 29–30,
109, 169

Macarius of Optino, Saint, 140
Magnificat, 175–76
Main, Dom John, 127
Manasseh, Prayer of, 114
Marcel, Gabriel, 139

Martyr, Justin, 134
Mary and salvation, 170–77
Mater Dolorosa, 175
maturation, spiritual, 37–38
McCabe, Herbert, 44–45, 110,
117
meaning, hunger for, 1
meditation, 8, 149
Merton, Thomas, 78, 133, 139
mindfulness, 149
Moses, 40
Mount Saviour Monastery
(Elmira, NY), 91–92, 94
mystery, divine, 3
mystical theology, 3–5, 14,
55–56, 90, 118

New Seeds of Contemplation
(Merton), 133
Nicene Creed, 9, 96
Nicodemus, 116
noncanonical sources, 174

On Prayer (Origen), 144
On Spiritual Friendship
(Aelred), 39
"ordinary time" experiences, 94
Origen of Alexandria, 134, 144
origin of universe, 51–52

paschal mystery, 89–90, 93,
107–9
passion of Jesus, 82–83
Pastoral Care (Gregory the
Great), 69–70
Paul, Saint: on baptism, 39, 50;
on church as body of Christ,
123, 128; to churches in Galatia, 70–71; on creation/resur-

rection, 85; on death, 155; on
fruit of the Spirit, 79–80; on
humility, 108; on prayer, 140,
142; and road to Damascus,
124–26; on Satan as angel of
light, 141; on sin and death,
101; on Spirit in our hearts,
79; and Stephen's death,
123–24; on suffering, 106–7;
and thorn in flesh, 70
Péguy, Charles, 117
Pentecost, 42, 172
Peter: sense of unworthiness
of, 28; and speech to Jewish
authorities, 9
Pharisee, in parable, 108
poverty, 55
prayer: answers to, 153–54;
dedicated time for, 148–49;
distraction and divine silence,
151–52; Frank's reflections on,
139–47; for God's will, 149–51;
impediments to, 140–42; Jesus
in garden of Gethsemane,
154; questions concerning,
148–54; with Scripture, 149;
theology, 3; transformative
power of, 147
prodigal son, 10, 108, 114–15

reconciliation, 97
redemption, 97
Reformation, the, 175
restlessness, 1, 28, 79
resurrection, 42, 68, 85–88,
91–95
revelation: Frank's reflections
on, 39–40; general, 38; mystery of, 39; special, 38

Revelations of Divine Love (Julian of Norwich), 145, 167
Rublev, Andrei, 49
Ruusbroec, Blessed Jan van,
47–48

sacraments, 135
salvation: faith in, 96–97; love's
story of, 100–103; and Mary,
170–77; origin of word, 97;
and self-giving, 103–10; sin's
story of, 98–100; the wonder
of God's acts, 96–98
Sarah, 49, 85
Satan, 28–29, 141–142. *See also*
devil
Scottish Episcopal Church
prayer, 169–70
Scripture, praying with, 149
Seeds of the Word, 134
self-agency and God, 112–13
self-giving: God's divine, 41–42,
51–52, 119; and salvation, 103–
10; self-giving love, 67–69, 98;
of the Trinity, 89
self-loss transformed into
self-giving love, 67–69
Shepherd of Hermas, The, 122
Showings (Julian of Norwich),
116, 145
silence from God, 45–46
sin, and story of salvation,
98–100
Society of Saint John the Evangelist, 137
solidarity in suffering, 69–71
spiritual consolation of Trinity,
45–47
spiritual dryness, 37, 151–52

Spiritual Exercises (Loyola), x,
142
Stephen, 123–25
Sub Tuum Presidium, 174
suffering: Frank's reflections on
solidarity in, 69–71; and God's
presence, 65–67; and human
evil, 64–65; hurtful ideas
about, 63–64; problem of
natural, 61–62; and resurrection, 67–69

tax collector, in parable, 108
Teilhard de Chardin, Pierre, 95,
132, 158, 161
theological virtues, 25
theophany, 54, 59
Theotokos, Mary as, 174, 177
Thomas Aquinas, Saint:
analogy of artisan, 55; God as
cause of all things, 54–55; on
God's presence, 52; Jesus as
Word become flesh, 36
Traherne, Thomas, 57–58,
162–64

tribal gods, 32–33
Trinity: and grace, 117–20;
mystery of, 41–50; and personal transformation, 48–50;
Ruusbroec's vision, 47–48;
and salvation, 97; for spiritual
consolation, 45–47; Trinitarian rhythm, 89; within every
being, 55

Underhill, Evelyn, 167

Walking on Water (L'Engle), 10
Weil, Simone, 46–47, 89, 169
white stone, book of Revelation, 162
Williams, Rowan, 128
Word: and Godself, 15; Incarnate, Jesus as, 72–81; Seeds
of, 134

"Ye Watchers and Ye Holy
Ones" (hymn), 177

Zacchaeus, 72

Index of Scripture

OLD TESTAMENT

Genesis
1:25	59
26:18	134

Exodus
3:14	6

Deuteronomy
30:14	40

Job
42:5–6	160

Psalms 59–60
19:1	132
27:8	143
37:9	159
95:7	40
119:71	93
139	60–61

Isaiah
55:8	116
55:8–9	161

NEW TESTAMENT

Mark
3:21	172
14:36	105

Luke 130
1:46–48	170–71
1:46–55	175–76
18:9–14	108
21:19	107

John 1
1:3–4	131
1:16	131
3:8	116
3:16	146
10:10	106

10:17–18	105
12	2
12:24	107
14:1–2	158–59
15:4	131
15:13	68, 104
16:12	40

Acts 9, 123
9:1–19	124

Romans
4:17	85
5:3–5	106–7
5:20	116
8:15–16	104
8:26	139
8:26–27	142
8:29	94, 114
8:38–39	156
12:2	145

1 Corinthians

12:4–7	127
12:16–17	128
12:24–26	128
13:12	155, 159, 167
15:50–53	156

2 Corinthians 123

3:17	60, 92, 109
5:17	125
5:19	96
6:10	60
11:14	141

Galatians

1:13–14	123
1:14	142
2:20	135
5:1	60, 109, 134
6:2	70–71

Ephesians 156

3:8	40, 133
4:11–16	131
4:15	172

Colossians

2:12	107

Hebrews 22, 23

1:3	60, 131
2:14–15	100–101, 102
11:1	23
11:8–16	22–23

1 John 4, 78

3:2	157
4:7	127
4:16	126

Revelation

2:17	157
12:10	141

DEUTEROCANON-ICAL BOOKS

Wisdom of Solomon

7:24	131
13:3	9

PSEUDEPIGRAPHA

Infancy Gospel of James 174